# GALVESTON

# GALVESTON

INCLUDES

CLEAR LAKE/NASA,

KEMAH,

SEABROOK,

BRAZOSPORT AREA,

AND THE

BOLIVAR PENINSULA

GAIL DRAGO

**Lone Star Books®**
A Division of Gulf Publishing Company
Houston, Texas

Selected material in this travel guide is provided courtesy of Sidewalk Houston, Microsoft Network's continually updated online guide to the city's arts and entertainment scene, leisure-time activities, and shopping options. Access the Houston site at http://houston.sidewalk.com.

# GALVESTON
## Includes Clear Lake/NASA, Kemah, Seabrook, Brazosport Area, and the Bolivar Peninsula

Copyright © 1999 by Gulf Publishing Company, Houston, Texas.
All rights reserved. This book, or parts thereof, may not be reproduced in any form without express written permission of the publisher.

Gulf Publishing Company
Book Division
P.O. Box 2608 □ Houston, Texas 77252-2608

10   9   8   7   6   5   4   3   2   1

**Library of Congress Cataloging-in-Publication Data**

Drago, Gail, 1947–
    Lone Star Guide: Galveston, includes Clear Lake/NASA, Kemah, Seabrook, Brazosport Area, and the Bolivar Peninsula
        p.   cm. — (Lone star guides series)
    Includes index.
    ISBN 0-89123-038-6 (alk. paper)
    1. Galveston Region (Tex.)—Guidebooks.   2. Galveston Island (Tex.)—Guidebooks.   I. Title.   II. Series.
F394.G2D73   1998
917.64' 130463—dc21                                        98-17383
                                                              CIP

Printed in the United States of America.

Printed on acid-free paper (∞).

Book design by Roxann L. Combs.

Cover design by Senta Eva Rivera.

*Dedicated to my son*
Nicholas Dean Drago

# CONTENTS

# ACKNOWLEDGMENTS

Many helped me with this endeavor. Special gratitude goes to Robert Warren, Christine Hopkins, and Ann Basurto of the Galveston Convention and Visitors Bureau. I also wish to thank Dancie Ware and Leslie Friedman of Dancie Perugini Ware Public Relations, who provided me with reams of information. As for Kristine Fahrenholz, my editor, your expertise added so much to the final product.

As for Anthony, my husband, and Nick, my son, thanks for your continued support. Once again during the Christmas holidays you helped me to meet a deadline. Let's hope that this summer we can spend some leisure time together in Galveston!

# About the Author

Native Texan **Gail Drago** has been a freelance writer for more than 15 years. Her articles have appeared in *Houston City* magazine, *Millionaire,* and the now-defunct *Houston Post.* In addition, she has co-authored *Texas Bed and Breakfast, Texas Historic Inns Cookbook, Outlaws in Petticoats and Other Notorious Women of Texas,* and *Etta Place—Her Life and Times with Butch Cassidy and the Sundance Kid.* When not writing about Texas, Gail teaches high school English and lectures on Texas travel and western history.

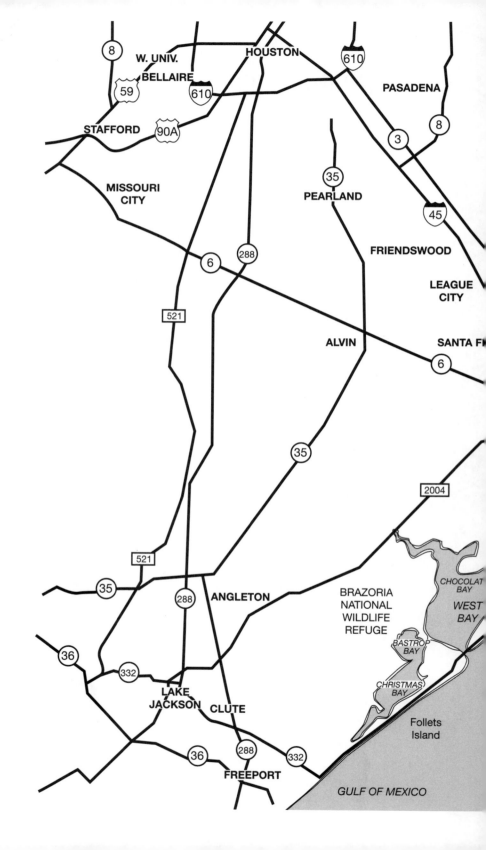

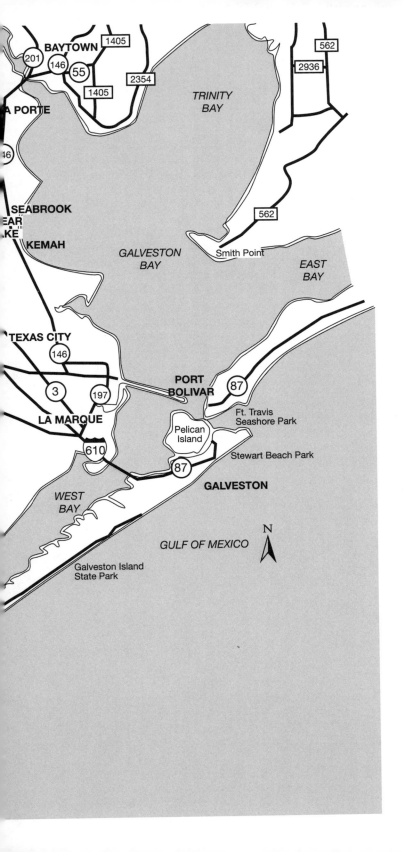

# Introduction

## Galveston: The Oleander City

Known affectionately as the "Oleander City" for its abundance of that flower, Galveston Island always has held a summer spell, particularly for us who call the Gulf Coast *home*. From its long stretch of beach with spiraling gulls and romantic Seawall to the historic houses that reign along Broadway Boulevard, the island, in my childhood, was a mystical seaside retreat reached by driving southwest down the now-closed Highway 87 along the coastline from Port Arthur and then taking the Bolivar ferry. With my father at the wheel of our wood-paneled station wagon and my mother beside him, my brother and I could hardly harness our excitement as we approached the lighthouse and then the ever-present line of cars in wait at the peninsula dock. When it was finally our turn, we boarded the vessel and rode across Galveston Bay. It was our tradition to stand at the bough as we braved the strong salty winds whipping our hair. When the short trip was over and our car rumbled off the ferry and onto the island, I knew we had reached our Texas paradise at last.

That was a long time ago, but I can still remember hastily pulling off my sandals as we approached Stewart Beach. As soon as my father turned off the engine, we would fling open the doors and race toward the churning waves. It's a ritual I still repeat today, forty-five years later.

But Galveston's charm goes far beyond the surf curling under cloudless skies, for it has grown into an arresting city, nurtured by native sons and rooted in the sand by a  history all its own. Whatever the event, whether it be pirate occupation, a great fire, or the deadliest hurricane in American history, Galveston Island and its people represent the human spirit at its strongest.

# GALVESTON

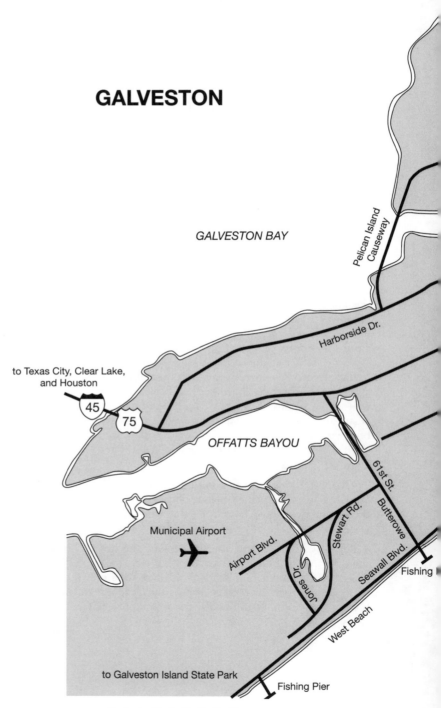

*GALVESTON BAY*

Pelican Island Causeway

Harborside Dr.

to Texas City, Clear Lake, and Houston

45

75

*OFFATTS BAYOU*

61st St.

Municipal Airport

Airport Blvd.

Stewart Rd.

Butterowe

Jones Dr.

Seawall Blvd.

Fishing

West Beach

to Galveston Island State Park

Fishing Pier

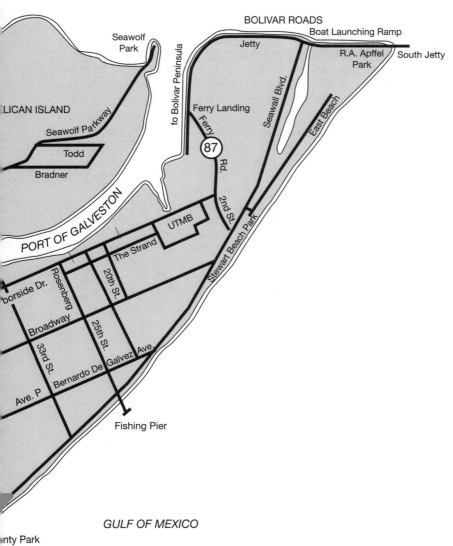

# THE ISLAND TODAY

Located on the Gulf of Mexico, 50 miles south of Houston, Galveston is a 32-mile-long semi-tropical barrier reef island that averages two miles in width and offers its entire Gulf Coast beach to visitors. On its jagged side, it parallels the coast, two miles away, while on the other, its boundary runs straight along the surf.

Residents of this very popular resort expect 42 to 47 inches of rainfall per year and a mild climate with water temperatures that vary from 57°F in winter to 81°F in summer. Breezes blow from the southeast except in winter months when wind rushes from the north. In summer, Galveston is cooler than most of Texas although in the winter, "blue northers" can sweep through to frost the island and plunge thermometer readings to 20°F. The peak season makes up for any wintry discomfort, however, for the spring brings clear azure skies over rolling seas. For this reason, summer weekends are crowded, particularly during holidays, with long lines at popular sights and restaurants. Obviously, the best time to visit the island is midweek.

For those "Born on the Island (BOI)," Galveston means "their" home, a place they loved long before the throng of tourists began flooding to their island. Proud of local history, however, they welcome vacationers ready to "taste the fruits" of a city experiencing a modern-day renaissance. As for BOIs, most come from hardy stock, a people who consider hurricane season a yearly inconvenience. With saltwater in their veins, these islanders simply don't cower even to the most formidable of forecasts.

Take, for example, Galvestonians of a century ago. Most of those who survived the Great Storm of 1900 chose to rebuild the flattened city known before the devastation as the "Queen of the Gulf." To protect the island, which is only 4.5 feet above sea level, city fathers built a 17-foot-high, 10-mile-long seawall while an astounded nation watched. Completed in 1907, the meandering concrete structure has since saved countless lives from future hurricanes. In spite of best efforts, though, Galveston Island never regained its original luster. After the great tidal wave, it dozed in the shadow of Houston, its sister city reaping the spoils of commerce needed for the island to rise once again as a leading Texas city.

More recently, however, with the help of some very influential citizens, a rebirth has occurred with major focus on The Strand, a National Landmark District. The beaches have also been replenished with sand, and luxurious new hotels and restaurants continue to sprout in the sand. And, as if hearing the call, tourists, historians, medical students, businessmen, entrepreneurs, and sportsmen alike make their way daily over the causeway to benefit from the Island.

A monthly diet of festivals has also contributed to island growth. The city's calendar is packed with such events as Mardi Gras, Dickens on the Strand at Christmas, the Historic Homes Tour, and the Fourth of July celebration. Even during non-festival season, tourists see literally hundreds of attractions from museums to more than 550 landmarks, many Greek Revival, Romanesque, and Italianate mansions, to Moody Gardens to the magnificent Tall Ship *Elissa*. As for accommodations, Galveston Island tourists choose from 3,400 rooms offered by hotels and the thriving bed-and-breakfast industry. For those who like ultimate privacy, literally hundreds of beach houses and condominiums can be rented for rates that vary from season to season. Known as a year-round resort, the target market is as varied as the attractions, with families, sportsmen, festival goers, movie directors, "winter Texans," and the convention and corporate crowd heading for the Island.

And no wonder they all come, with the Strand National Historic Landmark District, encompassing more than 100 shops, restaurants and art galleries, the University of Texas Medical Branch and Texas A&M University at Galveston, a choice of consumption and non-alcoholic beaches, and 15 museums including the new Ocean Star Offshore Energy Center, the Texas Seaport Museum, and the Lone Star Flight Museum. With its spectacular Rainforest Pyramid, Ridefilm Theater, Palm Beach, and Discovery Museum, The Moody Gardens can keep a visitor busy all day while such attractions as Seawolf Park and the Mosquito Fleet add even more variety to a day of touring. As for theater, the musical and dramatic choices are vast from the historic 1894 Grand Opera House productions to those presented at the Mary Moody Northen Amphitheatre.

And the food? There's no better fare than that offered by Galveston restaurateurs. Every day local chefs receive at their back kitchen doors fresh Gulf catches just off commercial boats. In many locations, diners eat outdoors as soft breezes find their way through the island's oleander and palm trees, while at others, history permeates elegant decor.

Be forewarned that although the island has a string of beachfront hotels and condominiums along Seawall Boulevard, one should make reservations well in advance. Beach houses are also for rent on the west end of the Island in Pirate's Beach, Indian Beach, Jamaica Beach, and Sea Isle. Peak tourist times are the summer months, Mardi Gras, the historic Homes Tour in May, and the first weekend in December when the annual event, "Dickens-on-the-Strand," occurs. The key to having a good time is to plan ahead.

So, come to Galveston Isle and experience the serenity of the sea. Enjoy yourself for ". . . by the sea, time is always early." But if its bustling tourism is too much excitement, flip over to the pages in this guide for the quieter options of the Bolivar Peninsula, Brazosport, Kemah and Seabrook, and if you're scientifically minded, there's always NASA.

## Geographical Facts

- As a barrier island, Galveston helps protect the Texas coast.
- Galveston is located on northwest coast of the Gulf of Mexico, 345 miles west of the Mississippi River.
- Galveston is a migratory flyway; 2,000 ornithologists visit each year.

- The island helps to protect the coastline that has changed through the centuries because of man and hurricanes.
- Prevalent east-to-west currents bring silt, particles, and shells toward Galveston. As a result, waters are sometimes clouded with Mississippi "mud"; the water table lies within four feet of the surface and is brackish.
- The fine sand, which permeates the soil, is gray, brownish-gray, and pale yellow with no underlying bedrock.
- Once an attempt was made to establish another town at San Luis Pass, but the water was too shallow. It now serves as a tidal funnel, which is a natural path for receding tidal waters.
- Pelican Island, a small isle north of Galveston, was once a narrow marsh with a remnant of dry land in 1816. Catching silt over the years, it is now on solid ground and is an important roosting ground for seabirds.
- Galveston Bay, 17 miles wide and seven to eight feet deep, extends 30 miles northward and is irregularly shaped; Dickinson, Buffalo Bayou, Clear Creek, San Jacinto River, Trinity River, and Cedar Bayou all drain into it. Mud flats and salt marshes around the bay are botanical estuaries with many varieties of grasses rotted in brackish water. They are home to wildlife, which range from butterflies to blackbirds, spiders, snakes, alligators, and rattlesnakes.
- Bolivar Peninsula is to the north and separates East Bay from the Gulf of Mexico. The opening between the peninsula and the island is the main entryway into Galveston Bay and can be traversed via ferries.
- West Bay is a two-mile stretch located between Galveston Island and the mainland to the southwest.

## Galveston Island Convention and Visitors Bureau

2102 Seawall Blvd. • Galveston, TX 77550
888-GAL-ISLE or 409/ 763-4311
FAX 409/765-8611
web site: www.galvestontourism.com

## Strand Visitors Center

2016 Strand • Galveston, TX 77550
409/765-7834 • 281/280-3907 (Houston)

# ISLAND HISTORY—PAST AND PRESENT

Galveston's history is rich with events such as deadly storms, places like the Strand, and colorful characters like pirate Jean Lafitte and the dynamic Galvestonian, Bettie Brown, who entertained Galveston society at her elegant Ashton Villa. But the story that revolves around the island's birth began 180 million years ago in the middle of the Mesozoic Era when it appeared in the Gulf of Mexico. Through the centuries sedimentary deposits, sand, gravel, and shells collected through the Cenozoic Era to create what is today the Houston, Galveston, Texas City landscape. Rich in natural resources, the geography here has given technological advantage in the way of oil, gas, salt, sulfur, harbors, and rivers to the Lone Star State.

The first men to know Galveston were the Karankawas, a towering tribe of Indians who spent winters on the island and summers on the mainland. They were not a pretty sight. Ill-kept, they covered themselves with shark's oil and alligator grease to repel clouds of mosquitoes and chewed tar balls. The men went naked while women of the tribe wore Spanish moss. They completed their look with braided hair tipped with snake rattles. Their diet was as suspect as their looks as some historians believe that the Karankawas sometimes devoured human flesh, although their main source of food consisted of deer, fish, oysters, turtles, berries, nuts, and persimmons. The historical community is still undecided in regard to their cannibalistic tendencies, but it is believed that tribal members stood about seven feet tall.

There's little doubt the ship-wrecked Spanish explorer **Cabeza de Vaca** was apprehensive when, in 1528, he met this strange little band, covered with blue tattoos and with lips pierced with canes, as they came ashore. This island experience proved unpleasant for the captain and crew as it wasn't long before mosquitoes attacked. Without hesitation, de Vaca dubbed the place "Malhado," the isle of doom. After six years and with only de Vaca and three other survivors left, the four walked into northern Mexico, happily returning to civilization and bringing Spanish authority with them. As for the Karankawas, little did they know that this first meeting with western man would be the beginning of their end. Because of wars with pirates, coupled with the tolls of a primitive lifestyle, the tribe was extinct by the mid 1800s.

By the mid 1700s, **Cavalier Sieur de la Salle**, representing France, had visited the island and named it *San Luis*, in honor of his French sovereign. However by 1777, both Texas and Mexico came under Spanish claim and **Count Bernardo de Galvez**, viceroy of Mexico under Spain, ordered the first survey of Galveston Bay. Galveston was named in his honor although he never set foot there. By 1816, **Louis-Michel Aury**, an independent naval commander commissioned by Mexico, was instructed to claim the pirate-ridden Galveston as part of the Republic of Mexico. He turned this noble order into self-promotion and reaped the benefits of privateering himself. After being unsuccessful, though, he moved on, leaving Galveston Island to the notorious **Jean Lafitte**, "Pirate of the Gulf," as self-proclaimed ruler.

In 1817, Galveston, a small settlement, was yielding to the formidable Lafitte who had gained his temporary nobility by fighting in 1815 for General Andrew Jackson in the Battle of New Orleans. He declared himself "governor" of the town he named *Campeche*, and for a time, he and more than 2,000 other pirates lived on the land where the University of Texas Medical Center (UTMB) campus is now. Having put in his "straight" time by supporting Andrew Jackson in his defeat of the British during the War of 1812, Lafitte resorted to his notorious ways and took advantage of Jackson's permission to seize enemy vessels by looting them for his own gain. It wasn't long before Campeche was the site of a large slave market, boarding houses for visiting buyers, a shipyard, saloons, pool halls, gambling houses, and Lafitte's own mansion, the "Maison Rouge."

After Lafitte's attack on an American ship, he was forced to abandon his operations in May, 1821, and the island fell to the U.S. Navy, which put up quite a fight against the thriving band of well-armed pirates. Before leaving, Lafitte held a huge party with wine and whiskey for his smugglers and then burned Campeche. Legend proclaims that before he left, he buried a treasure somewhere either on the peninsula or on Galveston Island. To date, it has never been found although treasure hunters have searched for over a century.

In 1836, four Texas Navy ships made headquarters on the Island and protected the Texas coast from harassment by the Mexican Navy. These ships prevented supplies and men from reaching Santa Anna, insuring victory for Sam Houston's army at San Jacinto, 22 miles northwest of Galveston. Once Texas became a republic in 1836, **Michel B. Menard,** a native of Canada, purchased seven square miles of land for $50,000 from the Austin Colony to establish the city of Galveston. Adding money and support were nine investors, including Gail Borden, Jr., condensed milk inventor; Samuel May Williams, "Father of the Texas Navy;" and John Allen, one of the two brothers who founded Houston. From there, Galveston grew and eventually became a prime example of the fruits of the "Gilded Age." Fortunes were made, and mansions sprouted along Broadway Boulevard and the Silk Stocking District, where wealthy businessmen could afford to purchase expensive silk stockings for their wives.

Incorporated in 1839, the island soon became the "Gateway to Texas." It also carried the new title of "Little Ellis Island," for Italian, German, Russian, Polish, and French immigrants began pouring into Texas to begin new lives. But while immigrants came in, products were being exported through its bustling harbor via scores of ships from all over the world. The media was a measuring stick for its success, for not only did local newspapers record the island's financial growth, but between 1838 and 1842, 18 newspapers were also born. One such paper was the *Galveston News*, founded in 1842, the only surviving paper of its day in Texas, which is now published as the *Galveston County Daily News*.

Opening the island for railroad expansion, a bridge to the mainland was finished in 1860. The Civil War came and went with the city's movers-and-shakers holding steadfast to their newly-made fortunes. With cotton as king, Galveston's golden years lasted until 1900. Wholesalers, merchants, bankers, fishermen, cotton agents, and retailers built their businesses as insurance companies and the shipping industry enjoyed "high cotton." The Strand, dubbed the "Wall Street of the Southwest," was a financial hubbub where such noted citizens as John Sealy, William Moody, Walter Gresham, James Moreau Brown, and Henry Rosenberg made Galveston history. As for the island, it became known as the second richest city in the United States and the most financially blessed in Texas.

# Great Storm of 1900

Just as Houston began to bow to its nemesis, Galveston felt the rage of nature, which took the form of a giant hurricane. In the early morning hours of September 8, 1900, heavy winds and rain began to pound at the flat-terrained island, where sand dunes had been removed to improve access to the beach. The city was only 4.5 feet above sea level with the highest altitude, around 14th and Broadway, at 8.5 feet. By 5 p.m. that evening, winds whipped up to 84 miles per hour with gusts over 100 miles per hour. By 7:30 p.m. that evening, a great tidal wave hit the island's south shore, ripping houses from their foundations and sending them crashing into the sea.

Many took refuge at the Tremont Hotel while others found safety at some of the Broadway Boulevard mansions and Jesuit College. Those huddled inside heard people screaming for help, but they all knew the situation was out of their control. When the winds finally calmed and the deep waters returned to sea, the island was in total devastation. Among the debris lay thousands of bodies. Some victims were never recovered. For at least one month after the storm, workers uncovered the dead at a rate of 70 per day. Of the original 38,000 island population, 6,000 people had been killed, and the Great Storm of 1900 was declared the worst natural disaster in American history.

Makeshift morgues were set up, but there were too many bodies. Survivors loaded the victims onto wagons and then barges and took them out to sea. However, the tides returned the dead back to shore, causing a tremendous health problem. Finally, having no other choice, the survivors burned the bodies in the funeral pyres or buried them in massive graves. Soon after the storm, tired workers were horrified to discover a string of drowned orphans tied to a dead Catholic sister from St. Mary's Orphanage.

The 1900 Storm and the opening of the Houston Ship Channel in 1908 ended Galveston's control over the Texas waterways. But residents prided themselves with their heads "bloodied but unbowed." In an unprecedented move, the Corps of Engineers dredged in tons of sand, raising the island by 12 feet. Many structures were jacked up during the grade raising, with some mansions, including Ashton Villa, saved by filling their basements. During the eight-year process, residents used elevated wooden sidewalks to walk through town. Began in 1902, the project was completed in 1910 and included 500 city blocks.

In a move that marked the island's renaissance, the Corps of Engineers also built a 10-mile-long, 17-foot-tall granite, sandstone, and concrete seawall. This project took seven years, and today Galveston's Seawall now extends 54,790 feet, one-third of Galveston's ocean front. Total cost was $14,497,399. Coupled with the building of Hotel Galvez, Galveston Island was on its way to recovery.

Unfortunately, with Houston's port benefiting by the island's recuperation period, the fledgling island port turned into the island's red-light district. Concentrated on Postoffice Street west of 25th, the houses of prostitution played host to a varied clientele from foreign sailors to big name businessmen. By the 30s and 40s, there were more prostitutes per citizen in Galveston than in Shanghai. Prohibition gave birth to bootlegging in the 20s and 30s, and the "speak-easies" brought shady excitement to the city with liquor supplied by European sources. Booze was shipped to the island via "rum row," and the use of speed boat crews to offload booze from ships anchored in international waters. Nightlife was anything but dull on Postoffice Street.

Although prohibition was repealed in 1933, liquor by the drink was illegal in Texas until 1971. It was during this time that a pair of Italian businessmen, brothers Sam and Rose Maceo, opened the first air-conditioned gambling house in the country, the Hollywood Dinner Club, a nationally acclaimed "dining" establishment that brought such big name entertainers to the island as Duke Ellington, Freddy Martin, Paul Whitman, Guy Lombardo, Phil Harris, and Spike Jones. The Maceos were wise in the ways of public relations and actively campaigned to gain local approval. They organized free seaside public concerts featuring stars straight from Hollywood and Vegas, and they supported showy bathing beauty contests. The Maceos always supported local causes. As a result, their Hollywood Dinner Club and later, in the 40s, their stylish over-the-water Balinese Room, haven for high rollers from out of state and neighboring cities flourished in spite of state officials who raided regularly and with no success.

In the late 50s, a less tolerant state attorney general, together with the Texas Rangers, came in with guns blasting. They found 550 slot machines hidden at Bolivar Point's Fort Travis which Wilson's men destroyed in front of news cameras. One thousand more machines, including pinball machines hidden in the closed Hollywood Dinner Club, were smashed, burned or dumped into the harbor.

When the sand settled, Galveston's adult playground was closed and the island seemed to drift off into a long slumber. Galveston's low profile lasted over 30 years until Galvestonian, oil tycoon George Mitchell, together with the Galveston Historical and the Moody Foundations, decided to revitalize the island. Within ten years, the 1894 Grand Opera House was restored and the Tall Ship *Elissa* was moored at Pier 21. The Tremont House was built, and the Mary Moody Northen Amphitheater brought summer theater-goers to the island. Restoration of the Strand, a monumental feat, went into full gear and today provides a colorful setting for the Christmas festival, "Dickens on the Strand," and Galveston's annual Mardi Gras. The Strand National Historic Landmark District is now home to more than 100 shops, antique stores, restaurants and art galleries, and museums. There are 550 designated historical landmarks on the National Register of Historic Places and over 1,500 historic homes, many open for tours. In addition, two other historic neighborhoods, including the East End Historic District and the Silk Stocking District, draw visitors each year.

With so many attractions, a rich history, a supportive population, and quality marketing strategies, Galveston is destined to be "Queen of the Gulf" once again.

# FIRST ON THE SCENE

The Galveston Historical Foundation, the state's second largest historic preservation group, recently celebrated its 125th anniversary. It has much to preserve as the following list will testify, for as Galveston grew, it became the site of many Texas "firsts":

- first post office (1836)
- first naval base (1836)
- first bakery (1838)
- first chapter of the Masonic Order (1840)
- first military company (1841)
- first cotton compress (1842)
- first law firm west of the Mississippi River (1846)
- first Catholic convent (1847)
- first cathedral (1847)
- first grocery store (1851)
- first railroad locomotive (1852)
- first insurance company (1854)
- first use of telegraph (1854)
- first private bank (1854)
- first jewelry store (1856)
- first gas lights (1856)
- first real estate firm (1857)
- first opera house (1870)
- first cotton exchange (1872)
- first orphanage (1876)
- first telephone (1878)
- first electric lights (1883)
- first black high school (1885)
- first medical college (1864)
- first electric street cars (1893)
- first school for nurses (1894)
- first golf course (1898)
- first country club (1898)

# GALVESTON ISLAND CALENDAR

The following calendar includes monthly events, estimated dates, and contacts. Theater performances are presented monthly by **Lone Star Performing Arts Association**, which sponsors the **Galveston Island Outdoor Musicals** (409/737-3440), staged at the **Mary Moody Northen Amphitheater**, the **Strand Theatre** (409/763-4591), the **Galveston Ballet** (409/763-8620), the **Galveston Symphony Orchestra** (409/762-2787), and the **Upper Deck Theatre** (409/744-9661). Mardi Gras and Dickens-on-the-Strand events are listed in the Festivals section. As for year-round events, including the **Galveston ArtWalk**, the **Ridley Sea Turtle Tours**, the **Dolphin Watch** and those planned for **Moody Gardens**, see separate listing that follows:

## JANUARY

**Wiener Dog Nationals**, one of Gulf Greyhound Park's biggest annual promotions, brings giggles to the crowd as these determined hot dogs race with short little legs at top speeds to the finish line. Call 800-ASK-2WIN.

**The Civil War Weekend** revolves around Union and Confederate encampments, a reenactment of the Battle of Galveston, as well as special tours, lectures, and exhibits. All activities take place on Galveston's historic waterfront and locations throughout the Island. Call the Galveston Historical Foundation (409/765-7834).

**Galveston Historical Foundation's Annual Sacred Places Tour**, sponsored by the Galveston Historical Foundation, takes visitors to a number of historic churches in late January. Tickets are sold the day of the tour, which usually begins at Moody Memorial First United Methodist Church, 2805 53rd St. Call 409/765-7834 or 281/280-3907 for details.

# FEBRUARY

**Mardi Gras! Galveston**, a 12-day event presented by the Galveston Park Board of Trustees and 14 participating krewes, is the traditional festival of merrymaking preceding the season of Lent. Celebrated with parades, masked balls, art exhibits, sporting events, and live entertainment, Mardi Gras brings almost one million people to the Island. Call 888/GAL-ISLE or 409/763-4311. (*See Mardi Gras section for event listings.*)

# MARCH

**Galveston Home and Garden Show**, Galveston Island Convention Center at Moody Gardens, One Hope Blvd., showcases 200 exhibits with everything from decorative items and gourmet fare to lawn tools. Almost 200 exhibits are featured. Proceeds benefit the Galveston Animal Shelter. Call 409/744-7848.

**March Madness Finals**, which parallel the NCAA Basketball Championship Tournament, is a Gulf Greyhound Park elimination stakes race series where top greyhounds compete in a two-dog, one-on-one championship race. Call 409/986-9500 or 800/ASK-2WIN.

**Explorer's Apprentice Camp: Rainforest Eggstravaganza**, Moody Gardens on One Hope Blvd; involves all ages from pre-school children to adults in an egg hunt through the rainforest. Call 409/744-4673 or 800/582-4673.

**Seawolf Park Drum Tournament**, Seawolf Park. Prizes awarded for the largest legal Drum, by weight. 409/744-5738.

**Academy Awards Ceremony Champagne Party**, Strand Theatre, 2317 Ship's Mechanic Row. Call 409/763-4591.

**Gulf Coast Volleyball Association Spring Break Tournament**, Stewart Beach, Seawall and Broadway. Offers divisions for men, women, and mixed for all skill levels. Ratings and ranks are determined for local players who want to participate at national events. Call 281/482-1376.

**Annual Grand KIDS Festival,** 1894 Grand Opera House, 2020 Postoffice. A celebration of family and folk arts, features live entertainment. Unique booths offer "hands on" activities to children. Call 409/765-1894 or 800/821-1894.

**King and Queen Classic,** Gulf Greyhound Park, highlights the top male athletes against the top female athletes to see who is going to be the top reigning royalty. Call 800-ASK-2WIN.

**Party in the Park, Saengerfest Park,** 23rd and Strand. Live entertainment 1 p.m.–5 p.m. Call the Historic Downtown/Strand Partnership at 409/763-7080.

**Gulf Coast Volleyball Association Beach Blast Tournament,** Stewart Beach, Seawall and Broadway. Offering divisions for men, women, and mixed for all skill levels. Ratings and ranks are determined for local players who want to participate at national events. Call 281/482-1376.

**Annual "Easter Eggstravaganza," Saengerfest Park,** 23rd and Strand, and Phoenix House, 214 Tremont (23rd Street). A family fun-filled day includes an Easter Parade, Peter Rabbit, decorated egg contest, and an Easter egg hunt. Festivities begin at 1 p.m.

**"A Hoppin' Good Easter at the San Luis,"** San Luis Resort and Conference Center, 5220 Seawall. Easter Egg Hunt at 10 a.m., live bunnies flower show by the Garden House, kite demonstrations by Kites Unlimited, Easter crafts and more. Bunny Brunch—eat with the Bunny, get his autograph, and have picture taken with him. Call 409/744-1500.

**Migration Weekend Family Days,** Ocean Star Offshore Drilling Rig and Museum, Pier 20 and Harborside Drive. See the exciting display that leads into the museum featuring the resident bird population. Speakers from the Galveston Chapter of the Bird Society give lectures and show films about Texas birds. Drawing classes provided for children and adults teach the basics of sketching local birds. Call 409/766-7827.

**The Annual Upper Texas Coast Birding Festival,** the Galveston Island Hilton Resort, 5400 Seawall. This exciting festival provides an opportunity for participants to see over 200 species of birds. Participants go to the top birding locations in coastal East Texas for a cross-section of aquatic and terrestrial birds. Small groups are professionally guided through state parks, wildlife refuges, and other bird havens for three successive days. Call 409/737-4081.

**KiteFest,** Stewart Beach, Seawall and Broadway. Kite flying festival that includes sport kite demonstrations, including individual, 2-man, 4-man, and mega flyers. Large and exotic single-line kites from around the world. Candy drops from kites for kids. Hands-on teaching for anyone who wants to learn to fly a controllable kite. Demonstrations and buggy rides "powered" by 4-line ram airfoil kites which travel up to 30 mph. Call 409/762-1811.

**Annual Great Texas Birding Classic.** Entire Texas Coast, including Galveston. The biggest, longest, and wildest birdwatching tournament in the United States. Sponsored in part by the Galveston Island Convention and Visitors Bureau. Call Texas Parks and Wildlife at 888/TX-BIRDS.

# MAY

**Cinco de Mayo Beach Festival,** the first Sunday in May, is a Latin-flavored party on East Beach with live bands, fun, food, and activities. Call 409/762-EAST.

**Annual Galveston Historic Homes Tour,** first and second weekends in May, includes guided tours of Galveston Island's finest privately-owned historic residences. Tourists may purchase tickets at The Strand Visitors Center, 2016 Strand. Hosted by the Galveston Historical Foundation. Call 409/765-7834.

**Party in the Park, Saengerfest Park,** 23rd and Strand. Live entertainment 1 p.m.–5 p.m. Call the Historic Downtown/Strand Partnership at 409/763-7080.

**Magnificent Mother's Day Weekend,** San Luis Resort and Conference Center, 5220 Seawall. Mother's Day Special Package. On Saturday, mothers get pampered with manicures, pedicures, facials, and a health seminar. Special day classes for kids. On Sunday, Mother's Day awards and brunch. Call 409/744-1500.

**Red, White and Boom Weekend,** Strand Historical District. Free live entertainment throughout the day and fantastic fireworks wrap up the evening in a Memorial Day celebration. Sponsored by KHMX, 96.5. Call 888-GAL-ISLE.

**Annual Island Art Festival** showcases original art by Texas artists. An outdoor family event. 713/521-0133.

**Oleander Festival,** Moody Gardens, celebrates the official flowering plant of Galveston Island, known as "The Oleander City." This fragrant festival includes a floral design show and contest, an oleander exhibit, and a "Discovery Tent" for children and adults who like arts and crafts. Call 409/737-5435 or 409/762-9334.

**Annual Great Texas Birding Classic.** Entire Texas Coast, including Galveston. The biggest, longest, and wildest birdwatching tournament in the United States. Sponsored in part by the Galveston Island Convention and Visitors Bureau. Call Texas Parks and Wildlife at 888/TX-BIRDS.

**Galveston Island Outdoor Musicals** are sponsored by Lone Star Performing Arts. Mary Moody Northen Amphitheater. Summer shows vary from summer to summer but past performances include such favorites as *Oklahoma* and *My Fair Lady*. Call 409/737-3440 or 800/54-SHOWS.

**Gulf Coast Volleyball Tournaments,** Stewart Beach, occurs throughout the month, for the Gulf Coast Association men's and women's doubles. Call 713/482-1376.

**Texas National Jet Ski Competition,** beachfront along Seawall. The best in the world vie for the International Jet Ski Championship. One of a series of events of the International Jet Sports Boating Association, this challenging jet ski thriller pits man and machine against the roaring Gulf of Mexico. Call 409/762-3930.

**Spirit of Flight Air Show & Walkabout,** Lone Star Flight Museum, is an exciting air show featuring celebrity precision flying teams, plus the nation's finest restored warbirds reenacting historic events. Call 409/740-7722.

**Beachcombers Golf Tournament,** second week in May, begins with a Monday evening "Welcome Social," followed by Tuesday's mixed Florida Scramble and 54 holes with no elimination. Contact the Galveston Country Club for more information (409/763-8688).

**Annual Business Expo,** Moody Gardens, is sponsored by the Galveston Chamber of Commerce and features Galveston County businesses. Call 409/763-5326.

**Texas Crab Festival,** second weekend in May, Crystal Beach on Bolivar Peninsula. Crab races, a crab legs contest and crab cookoff and other family fun, including dancing, food, bands, crafts, and a seaside carnival. Call 409/684-3345, 800-SUN-FUN3.

**Family Day's Right on Course,** Texas Seaport Museum. A day when museum volunteers demonstrate traditional and electronic navigation techniques. All Family Day activities are included in the Seaport Museum's regular admission price. Call 409/763-1877.

**Texas Sprint Championship Qualifier Final,** Gulf Greyhound Park. Texas-bred greyhounds compete in an exciting tournament for the $75,000 purse. Call 409/986-9500, 800/ASK-2WIN.

**EarthFair,** mid May, Moody Gardens, celebrates Mother Earth with children and adult environmental workshops and activities. Call 800/582-4673.

**Memorial Day Classic,** Gulf Greyhound Park. Eight of the track's top greyhounds compete in a fast-paced "hot box" race.

**Opening of Palm Beach,** Moody Gardens, mid May. This is a chance to catch the first wave to Palm Beach, where guests of Moody Gardens plunge into a "Kick-off to Summer Mixer" with Mix 96 FM. Call 800/582-4673.

**KLOL Rocquafest,** East Beach, occurs in late May. Call 713/468-6824.

**Memorial Day Celebration,** Stewart Beach, is an invitation to all to join sun worshipers for a weekend of music, games, and prizes. Call 888/GAL-ISLE.

**Annual AIA Sandcastle Competition,** last weekend in May (or early June), East Beach. Sixty teams create incredible sandcastles in the largest sandcastle competition in Texas. Call 409/762-3278.

**Art Festival,** late May, Pier 21. This outdoor event showcases original works of artists from Galveston and all over Texas. The festival offers live entertainment, a children's "hands-on" art station, tasty delights supplied by the Island's finest restaurants, and a wine tasting table. Call 713/521-0133.

**Quilts in Motion: Annual Island Quilter's Guild Exhibit,** Galveston County Historical Museum, 2219 Market. Heirloom, modern, and miniature quilts will be on display on giant mobiles from the museum's 45-foot vaulted ceiling. End of month week-long event. Call 409/766-2340.

# JUNE

**Galveston Summer Band Concerts**, every Tuesday evening through June, July, and August, Sealy Park, 24th and Avenue I behind Ashton Villa, 7:30 p.m. The 20-member band provides family musical entertainment, including attractions for children. Call 409/744-2174. (The 1998 season marks their 70th anniversary.)

**Party in the Park, Saengerfest Park**, 23rd and Strand. Live entertainment 1 p.m.–5 p.m. Call the Historic Downtown/Strand Partnership at 409/763-7080.

**Annual AIA Sandcastle Competition**, early June (or last weekend in May), East Beach. Sixty teams create incredible sandcastles in the largest sandcastle competition in Texas. Call 409/762-3278.

**Gulf Coast Volleyball Tournaments**, Stewart Beach, happen throughout the month. The Gulf Coast Association season schedules men's and women's doubles. Call 713/482-1376.

**Backyard Garden Tour**, usually held at the beginning of June, this tour takes nature lovers to six of Galveston's most prestigious, private backyard semi-tropical gardens. Visitors get gardening tips from the owners. Proceeds benefit Clean Galveston. Call 409/762-3363.

**Galveston Island Outdoor Musicals** are sponsored by Lone Star Performing Arts. Mary Moody Northen Amphitheater. Summer shows vary from summer to summer but past performances include such favorites as *Oklahoma* and *My Fair Lady*. Call 409/737-3440, 800/54-SHOWS.

**Texas Juvenile Stakes Semi-Finals and Finals**, Gulf Greyhound Park, focuses on Texas-bred "juvenile" greyhounds beginning their racing career in this unpredictable series. Call 409/986-9500 or 800-ASK-2WIN.

**Family Day's Watch on Deck**, Texas Seaport Museum, allows visitors to experience life on board the 1877 Tall Ship *Elissa*. All Family Day activities are included in the Seaport Museum's regular admission. Call 409/763-1877.

**Williams Home Herb Fair,** 1839 Samuel May Williams Home, 3601 Bernardo de Galvez (Avenue P), features cooking, craft, and gardening demonstrations. Herb vendors and exhibitors add to this educational experience. Free admission. Call 409/765-7834.

**Annual Caribbean Carnival Festival,** Kempner Park, 27th and Avenue O. A taste of the islands on the Gulf Coast. Enjoy costume parade, Caribbean market, Calypso and Steelband competition, arts, food, folkloric dancers, live entertainment, and limbo dances. Call the Galveston Caribbean Carnival Association at 409/643-7944.

# JULY

**Galveston Island Outdoor Musicals** are sponsored by Lone Star Performing Arts. Mary Moody Northen Amphitheater. Summer shows vary from summer to summer but past performances include such favorites as *Oklahoma* and *My Fair Lady.* Call 409/737-3440, 800/54-SHOWS.

**Galveston Summer Band Concerts,** every Tuesday evening through June, July, and August, Sealy Park, 24th and Avenue I behind Ashton Villa, 7:30 p.m. The 20-member band provides family musical entertainment, including attractions for children. (The 1998 season marks their 70th anniversary.) Features Patriot Day around July 4th. Call 409/744-2174.

**Family Day's Watch Below,** Texas Seaport Museum, allows visitors to learn about seaborne relaxation and nautical crafts. All Family Day activities are included in the Seaport Museum's regular admission price. Call 409/763-1877.

**Fourth of July Fireworks Display,** July 4th. Enjoy the annual fireworks display that lights up the Gulf in celebration of the 4th. Sponsored by the Galveston Park Board of Trustees. Sky gazers may park anywhere from 38th St. and Seawall Blvd. Display occurs around 9 p.m. Call 888-GAL-ISLE (888/425-4753).

**Moody Gardens July Fourth Watermelon Fest and Ice Cream Crank Off,** Moody Gardens. Benefits the Hope Therapy Program. Contestants bring ice cream recipes to the "chilly cook-off." Visitors munch on ice-cold watermelon and join in potato sack and wheelbarrow races. Teams register by calling 800/582-4673, ext. 361.

**Fourth of July Celebration,** Stewart Beach. Join in the fun in the sun with a sandcastle competition, contests, and prizes. Call 888/GAL-ISLE.

**Gulf Coast Volleyball Tournaments**, Stewart Beach. Several men's and women's doubles tournaments occur throughout the month. Begins in the morning, usually around 9:30 a.m. Call 713/482-1376.

**Strand Theatre**, 2317 Mechanic, offers a gamut of specialty viewing film, including movies from the Cannes Film Festival, children's musicals, and other live performances. Call 409/763-4591.

# August

**Galveston Island Outdoor Musicals** are sponsored by Lone Star Performing Arts. Mary Moody Northen Amphitheater. Summer shows vary from summer to summer but past performances include such favorites as *Oklahoma* and *My Fair Lady*. Call 409/737-3440, 800/54-SHOWS.

**Family Day's Gone to Texas**, Texas Seaport Museum, teaches visitors about family histories and immigration. All Family Day activities are included in the Seaport Museum's regular admission. Call 409/763-1877.

**Gulf Coast Volleyball Tournaments**, Stewart Beach. Several men's and women's doubles tournaments occur throughout the month. Gulf Coast Association Season. Begins in the morning, usually around 9:30 a.m. Call 713/482-1376.

**Galveston Summer Band Concerts**, every Tuesday evening through June, July, and August, Sealy Park, 24th and Avenue I behind Ashton Villa, 7:30 p.m. The 20-member band provides family musical entertainment, including attractions for children. Call 409/744-2174. (The 1998 season marks their 70th anniversary.)

# September

**Gulf Coast Volleyball Tournaments**, Stewart Beach. Several men's and women's doubles tournaments occur throughout the month. Begins in the morning, usually around 9:30 a.m. Call 713/482-1376.

**Chihuahua World Cup**, Gulf Greyhound Park. See these pint-sized speedsters strut their stuff in this world-class event, as hundreds of area Chihuahuas take to the track. Call 800/ASK-2WIN.

# OCTOBER

**Downtown "Walk-About,"** a treasure hunt in the historic Downtown/Strand District, where walkers visit 25 participating merchants in the area for the chance to win wonderful prizes. Proceeds benefit Clean Galveston. Call 409/762-3363.

**Oktoberfest,** First Lutheran Church, Oktoberfest celebration with authentic German food, crafts, and an Oompah band from Germany. Call 409/762-8477.

**Harborfest Galveston** showcases the working waterfront and the industry system in Galveston. Exhibits, displays, entertainment, and demonstrations continue throughout the day. Sponsored by the Port of Galveston. Call 409/766-6119.

# NOVEMBER

**Texas Aviation Hall of Fame and Lone Star Flight Museum Day,** a homecoming celebration for the museum's historic aircraft collection following a national tour, the nation's finest restored vintage warbirds in action over Galveston Island. Call 409/740-7722.

**Gulf Greyhound Park Month-long Anniversary Celebration** is an activity-packed day filled with the Gordon Wood Memorial Race, Fan Appreciation Day, free giveaways, an annual Adoption Reunion Parade, free commemorative posters, and free anniversary caps. Also includes **Thanksgiving Day Classic.** Call 800-ASK-2WIN.

**Texas Fall Derby Finals,** Gulf Greyhound Park, La Marque. See Texas-bred greyhounds compete in this stakes series. Call 800-ASK-2WIN.

**Lighted Boat Parade.** Saturday after Thanksgiving. Call Historic Downtown Partnership at 409/763-7080.

**A Victorian Christmas Home Tour,** Friday evening before Dickens on the Strand, offers tours of beautifully decorated (in Victorian holiday style) private historical homes as visitors are taken from home to home by horse-drawn carriage. Christmas carolers add to the spirit. Buy tickets *early* (very limited number!) at The Grand 1894 Opera House. Hosted by the East End Historic District. Call 409/765-1894 or 409/763-5928.

**Dickens on the Strand,** first weekend in December, fills the streets with the holiday spirit. Everywhere costumed characters, glittering parades, exciting entertainers, and unique vendors assist the Galveston Historical Foundation in recreating Queen Victoria's London. Call 409/765-7834. (*See Festivals section for event listings.*)

**Moody Garden's Lights Up for the Holidays,** every Saturday during the holidays, with a giant poinsettia tree and entertainment by area choirs. Call 800/582-4673.

**New Year's Eve Extravaganza,** hosted by the San Luis Resort, 5222 Seawall, is an exciting way to bring in the new year! Call 409/744-1500 or 800/445-0090 for reservations.

**New Year's Gala,** the Strand Theatre, 2317 Ship's Mechanic Row. Party begins around 8:30 p.m. Call 409/763-4591 for reservations.

**Aurevoir Race,** Gulf Greyhound Park, is a competition of top greyhounds that compete in this Hot Box event. Mandatory pay-outs on all jackpots. Call 800/ASK-2WIN or 409/986-9500.

*The IMAX Nutcracker,* Moody Gardens. The age-old Tschaikovsky ballet told in 3D and six stories high. This century-old story is a dream-like tale of the mystical sugarplum fairy, the villainous Mouse King, the hero Nutcracker himself, and other whimsical characters that help to bring Tschaikovsky's music to life. Call 800/582-4673 or 800/744-4673.

For more information contact the **Galveston Island Convention and Visitors Bureau** at 409/763-4311, toll-free at 888-GAL-ISLE (888/425-4753) or visit the official **Galveston Island Web site** at www.galvestontourism.com.

# Year-Round Events

**The Galveston ArtWalk,** held every six weeks, is open house for many of Galveston's galleries in the Strand Historical District. Guests sip refreshments and partake in *hors d'oeuvres* while viewing art work and exhibits by local, national, and international artists. The Galveston Island Trolley provides free transportation from the Strand to Gallery Row (Postoffice Street) and the Galveston Arts Center, 2127 Strand. Call 409/763-2403.

**Ridley Sea Turtle Tour,** 4700 Ave. U, is supported by the National Marine Fisheries Service. By appointment only, this tour gives visitors a chance to view the endangered sea turtle and learn about research being done to protect the species. Call 409/766-3500.

**Moody Gardens** sponsors monthly events that revolve around the Rainforest Pyramid, the Discovery Museum, and the IMAX Ridefilm Theater. Call 800/582-4673 or 800/744-4673.

**Dolphin Watch.** Every Saturday, nature lovers can observe the dolphin in their natural habitat from aboard the *Seagull II,* a Galveston Harbor Tours vessel. Reservations are required. 409/765-1700.

---

*A note about island streets . . .*
Before you begin exploring Galveston, be aware that many streets have two names. Tremont Street, for example, is also known as 23rd Street. Moody Avenue is called 21st Street by some.

---

# GALVESTON ISLAND
BEACHES

The Island has 32 miles of beautiful public beaches, billed as "the clean-est on the Texas Gulf Coast." These city-maintained shorelines are also manned with lifeguards from the Galveston County Sheriff's Department Beach Patrol. Although safety and rescue services are available, the sea commands respect as its currents and uneven bottom can take even an experienced swimmer off-guard and pull him or her out to sea. Follow the posted signs, stay close to shore, and swim safe distances from piers and pilings to ensure a safe stay on the Island.

As for beach maintenance, Galveston Island has successfully completed its nourishment project and prides itself on being the state's first to replen-ish its coastline by adding as much as 150 feet of sand to beach width from 10th Street to 61st Street along Seawall Boulevard. Once limited to areas on the east end of the Island, beachcombers now have a variety of loca-tions to enjoy. For your convenience, beach and umbrella concessionaires now provide their services in many of the new beach areas, designated by City Council and the Galveston Park Board of Trustees as alcohol-free. With the exception of licensed concession areas, the ban also encompasses the Seawall as well.

Although all Galveston beaches are for public use, every area, of course, has something different to offer. As soon as you take the causeway over from the mainland via I-45, you'll see the signs for East and West beaches. You'll note right away that the closer you get to the east end of the island, the more populated. West Beach starts where the Seawall ends with Sea-wall Boulevard changing to FM 3005. Beach houses begin to crop up on the left with beach communities composed of permanent residents and rental properties. If you like more secluded conditions, you'll love it here. There are three Galveston County beach parks along the road that offer dressing rooms with showers and toilets, food concessions, playgrounds, and picnic areas. Horseback riding, parasailing, windsurfing, and other commercial beach activities are available in the peak season.

If you're an urban animal and like more excitement, you'll find yourself turning around and heading back toward the city's East beach. Several small beaches with bathroom facilities dot the Seawall area although some are reserved for surfers, who find themselves prohibited near the Jetties. The more family-oriented beach park seems to be **Stewart Beach Park,** located at the juncture of Broadway (Interstate 45) and Seawall boulevards. Operated by the City of Galveston Park Board of Trustees, this park features a pavilion with gift shops, concessions, restaurants, and a large bath house. Adjacent to the park are a carnival and water slide, bumper boats and cars, go carts, miniature golf, and amusement rides. Although this beach is always crowded, it is by far the kids' favorite. Chair, float, surrey, roller skate, surfboard, rollerblade, bike, and umbrella rentals are also available. Along the boulevard, tourists can rent bicycles, roller skates, surreys, as well as rafts and surfboards. Since there is no railing on the seawall, however, you'll want to ride or skate a safe distance from the edge.

## Stewart Beach Park

### 6th and Seawall Blvd. • 409/765-5023 • $5 per car

Galveston's premier family beach, Stewart Beach Park is regularly the site of family-oriented events, such as volleyball tournaments, sandcastle competitions, and concerts, throughout the summer, and all are sponsored by the Park Board. The park features a children's playground, umbrella and chair rentals, volleyball courts, an outdoor pavilion with a snack bar, souvenir shop, restrooms, and a bath house. In addition, Amaze'N Texas, a life-size human maze, the WaterCoaster (at intersection of Broadway and Seawall Blvd.) and Patio Bar, Bumper Boats, and the Stewart Beach Mini Golf Course all provide added fun for those who love amusement attractions. The park is open mid-March through mid-October from 8 a.m. to 6 p.m. weather permitting. Alcohol-free beach.

## R. A. Apffel Park (also called East Beach)

### Seawall and Boddeker Dr. • 409/762-3278, 409/762-EAST
### $5 per car

Another city recreation spot just east of Stewart Beach, Apffel Park has its own **Big Reef Nature Park** where bird watchers can catch a glimpse of their favorite local species. This one is popular with families, fishermen, and teenagers. The facility offers an outdoor pavilion with a bath house, public restrooms, concessions, game room, volleyball courts, laundry facilities, and a gift shop, as well as a boat launch, jetty, and surf fishing facilities. Live music, concerts, and an outdoor bar add to the entertainment most weekends during the summer. Alcohol consumption is allowed at this beach park. There are no RV hookups. The park is open mid-March through mid-October from 8 a.m. to 6 p.m. weather permitting. Take Seawall Boulevard to Boddeker Drive to reach this park, located at the southeast tip of the island.

## Dellanera RV Park

**Located on the west end of the Seawall at 7 Mile Rd. and FM 3005**
**409/740-0390 • $12 per night, $3 per day per car**

Dellanera Park offers a long, quiet stretch of shoreline for camping. Amenities here include umbrella/chair rentals, beach-side restrooms, bath house, children's play area, volleyball courts, picnic sites. The large pavilion has a grocery store, snack bar, restrooms and showers, laundry facilities, and a recreation room. Open year-round with 50 full hook-ups.

## Galveston County Beach Pocket Parks

**Number 1, FM 3005 (San Luis Rd.) at 7½ Mile Rd.; Number 2, 9½ Mile Rd. on FM 3005; and Number 3, 11 Mile Rd. on FM 3005**
**409/770-5355 • $5 per vehicle**

All parks include a pavilion with restrooms, showers, and a boardwalk with some featuring concession stands. Open 9 a.m. to 6 p.m.

## Galveston Island State Park

**FM 3005 • 409/737-1222 • $3 per person 13 and older**

Galveston Island State Park, located on the west side of the island outside Galveston's tourist-busy sector, is a 2,000-acre preserve which includes wetlands, salt meadows, beach, dunes, and coastal prairie. Migratory birds include cuckoos, warblers, tanagers, orioles, thrushes, buntings, and grosbeaks. Permanent residents here are the mockingbird, great blue heron, snowy egret, white ibis, mottled duck, bobwhite, morning dove, red-bellied woodpecker, starling, red-winged blackbird, house sparrow, seaside sparrow, marsh wren, meadowlark, horned lark, white pelicans, and 53 species of seagulls, as well as other coastal birds such as sandpipers, seagulls, plovers, rails, terns, and brown pelicans.

Campers and day trippers enjoy picnic tables, barbecue pits, and water and electrical hook-ups on all sites. The park is open year-round.

## Palm Beach at Moody Gardens

**Hope Blvd. • 409/744-PALM • $5 per person**

Palm Beach is a man-made white-sand and blue-lagoon entertainment center for families and young adults. Built in 1987 as part of Moody Gardens, this beach offers waterfalls, Jacuzzis, volleyball, paddle boats, a yellow submarine for kids, and concessions. Be advised, however, that no food, drinks, or lawn chairs may be brought in. Hours vary with the season. *The Colonel Paddlewheeler*, which offers day and dinner cruises, is docked behind the beach. (*For more information on Moody Gardens see the Attractions section.*)

## Seawolf Park

**Pelican Island via Seawolf Pkwy. (51st St.) • 409/744-5738**

Seawolf Park was built on an immigration station site and provides a three-story pavilion with a view of Galveston harbor, picnic sites, a playground area, with volleyball courts, and a fishing pier. A World War II submarine, the *USS Cavalla*, a destroyer escort, the *USS Stewart*, and other military hardware are on display and open for tours. Seawolf Park is available for company picnics, school field trips, and private parties. The park is open year-round from dawn to dusk. (*For more information on this park, see the section on attractions.*)

## West Beach

**FM 3005 (off Seawall Blvd. near San Luis Pass) Galveston, TX 77550**

Head west toward the end of Galveston Island on FM 3005 for miles of beaches that look private, but aren't. Pirate's Beach is a small residential area with a nice public beachfront used mainly by residents. Once you pass Jamaica Beach, notice the occasional wooden staircases and very small parking areas next to the dunes. Stay off the environmentally sensitive dunes—they've been know to house the occasional snake. The ritzy beach homes of Houston's rich and sometimes famous make for some interesting sightseeing. You can also rent beach houses along FM 3005. No lifeguards or beach patrols on this part of the island.

# KNOW THE DANGERS OF THE OCEAN

As drowning is the second leading accidental killer of Americans between the ages of 1 and 44, most drowning victims range from 15 through 19 with children four-years-old and younger making up the second highest group. However, whatever the age and the skill level, it is important to remember that the Gulf of Mexico and its tides are unpredictable when it comes to power. Above all, respect the "No Swimming" signs. City officials have posted these warnings because of strong currents, deep holes, jagged rocks, and sudden drop-offs. Life ring buoys are housed in brightly colored boxes at the end of each rock groin along the seawall.

The locations listed below are designated as safe swimming areas. These areas will be marked with signs, and most are protected by Beach Patrol lifeguards. A flag warning system indicates swimming conditions:

Red–Dangerous    Yellow–Use caution    Blue–Marine life (Jellyfish)

## Safe Swim Areas are as follows:

100 ft. west of 59th St. rock groin to 100 ft. east of 61st St. rock groin.

100 ft. west of 51st St. rock groin to 100 ft. east of 53rd St. rock groin.

100 ft. west of 47th St. rock groin to 100 ft. east of 49th St. rock groin.

100 ft. west of 33rd St. rock groin to the eastern boundary of Stewart Beach.

100 ft. west of 17th St. rock groin to 100 ft. of 21st St. rock groin.

100 ft. west of 10th St. rock groin to the eastern boundary of Stewart Beach.

## A Word about Rip Currents . . .

Gulf Coast rip currents, mistakenly called "undertow," flow along the bottom near the shore. They occur when many waves break in rapid succession near the shore causing water to collect on the beach faster than it can flow back out. When so much water collects, it flows out in a fast, narrow "rip" current that cuts a channel in the bottom. Once you get beyond the breakers, the channel widens suddenly, and the current fans out and gets weaker. This strong seaward movement can be a deadly killer as it can suddenly sweep an unsuspecting swimmer out to sea.

The first way to avoid a rip current, of course, is to not go out too far. However, if you ever find yourself caught in one, remember not to swim straight for the shore. Trying to fight the current will tire you out, and you'll be in "deep water" for sure. If you'll remember that the current is narrow and dies out beyond the breakers, you can swim parallel to the shore in the hope of swimming out of the weakening current. Once out, you can then swim to shore. If it is stronger, float with it until it dies out, and then head for dry land.

Also remember that strong rip currents move near jetties, groins, and piers, and that these water movements dig deep holes. Stay at least 100 feet away.

## Sand Bars and Holes

Waves dig deep holes in the ocean floor near the beach and may be several yards wide. They can form in very shallow water, which makes them hazardous to small children who could be swallowed up in seconds. As for sand bars and troughs, created by coastal natural processes near the shoreline, they also pose danger. The height of the bar and the depth of the troughs vary, but the water in the trough can drown you. Take a look at swimmers who are in waist-deep water. Be aware that they are probably on a sand bar and that the water is more than likely deep between them and you. Above all, don't try to reach the offshore sand bar.

*Ensure a good time for you and your family by being aware of a few safety tips:*

- Never swim alone.
- Stay in shallow water. If you can swim, don't venture out to water that is more than waist deep. If you can't swim, stay very near the shore.
- Don't swim if you feel ill or tired. Rough waves can rob anybody of energy.
- Don't drink or use drugs and swim.
- Don't swim in boating or surfing areas.
- Don't swim during a thunderstorm, strong wind, or rough tides.
- Watch your kids! Never leave them in the water without you.
- Be considerate of other swimmers.
- Swimming near lifeguards is always better than depending upon your own lifesaving skills.

## Sea Animal Savvy

Animals of the sea don't like to be bothered and will swim away or burrow themselves in the sand to avoid you. Marine life such as man-of-war or jellyfish pose particular threats to swimmers as contact with them can leave a nasty sting. So, keep your eyes open for whitish floating "balloons," some with tentacles, and quickly move yourself and your kids from its path. However, if one does bite or sting, run to a lifeguard if there is one. For minor contact, use meat tenderizer. If it's serious, of course, see a doctor. You may need a tetanus shot if you suffer a puncture. You may also need to be treated for an allergic reaction or with antibiotics to prevent infection.

## Sand Dunes

Sand dunes are creations of the ocean breezes that blow sand into dry mounds that act as barriers between the beaches and human habitation. Constantly dynamic, the dunes shift until fortified by the long, stubborn roots of vegetation. Sea oats, dove weeds, goatweeds, sunflowers, and other types of vegetation provide havens for beetles, grasshoppers, lizards, crabs, gophers, mice and rats, rabbits, birds, and katydids. A word of caution, however! Diamondback rattlers, who wish to remain anonymous, sleep within the bending weeds, so take a well-trodden path instead of the road "less-traveled." Local hospital officials say they treat bites from rattlers frequently, so play it safe. On a less serious note, pesky mosquitoes also live among the reeds. The less they are stirred the better.

# Saving Yourself from Sunburn

Use a high sun-protector factor (SPF), even on cloudy or overcast days. Remember that there is no such thing as a safe tan. Exposure to the sun is dangerous, prematurely ages, and can cause cancer. Sunburns are especially harmful to children as problems with premature skin aging and skin cancer possibly could be set in motion before a child turns ten-years-old. Doctors say that 50 percent of an individual's total lifetime exposure to harmful ultraviolet radiation occurs by age 18.

For that reason, it is recommended that those 18 and younger use sunscreen with a SPF of 15 to reduce the risk by 78 percent of developing skin cancer. One bad sunburn can double the risk of future skin cancer. Those who have suffered three or more blistering sunburns before the age of 20 have five times the risks of developing melanoma. If perspiring, reapply, and if you are a sun worshiper who jumps in and out of the water, reapply.

The University Cancer Center, which provides public service radio and television skin advisories, base their information from measuring the amount of sun-generated ultraviolet light four times a day. The center's findings follow:

- A child wearing a wet T-Shirt in the water is not protected from the dangerous, penetrating ultraviolet rays of the sun. They need sunscreen for protection.

- An existing, slowly acquired tan does not allow safer and longer exposure to the sun.

- A tan acquired from a sunless tanning product will not keep you from sun burning if you are exposed to the sun.

- Hats or caps and cover-ups will protect back and arms. Sunglasses are a must for protecting the eyes.

- The sun's rays are most harmful from 11 a.m. to 4 p.m.

## St. Mary's Emergency Room

St. Mary's Hospital Emergency Department, located on the east side of the hospital, is located on Sixth and Market. It provides medical, surgical, pharmaceutical and diagnostic facilities, as well as the latest in medical technology. Open 24 hours everyday of the year, patients find their care here officiated by a board-certified staff.

# POINTS OF INTEREST

Galveston's attractions, each very different from the next, give visitors endless choices of things to do. Beachcombers have 32 miles of coastline to explore. History buffs can travel back to the Victorian Era by visiting The Strand, the East End, and the Silk Stocking historic districts. Kids always find magic at Moody Gardens, a place of glass pyramids where butterflies fly free, and the amazing 3D IMAX. Sportsmen can cast their lines from piers, boats, or directly into the surf. Adults learn about every mode of transportation through the Lone Star Flight Museum, the Classic Car Museum, and the Tall Ship *Elissa*. Visitors may travel around the island by car, trolley, plane, carriage, boat or on foot. If you drive or walk, be aware that some of Galveston's streets sport two names. Water Street, for example, is also known as Avenue A.

The following symbols are used to give you some idea of entry fees although all are subject to change:

$ = $5 and under
$$ = $5 to $10
$$$ = $11 to $20
$$$$ = $20 and up

## Moody Gardens

**IMAX 3D Theater and Ridefilm Theater • Rainforest Pyramid Discovery Museum • Palm Beach • One Hope Blvd. • 800/582-4673, 800/744-4673 • http://www.moodygardens.com • $$ per attraction; $ for access to Palm Beach • Call for IMAX 3D showtimes; they usually begin at 11 a.m. and are shown every two hours.**

One of Galveston's most popular attractions, **Moody Gardens**, is a lush, subtropic environment, filled with an estimated 20,000 plants and trees of seasonal varieties that add spectacular color to stone pathways for walkers and bikers. This intriguing attraction features a 10-story, 40,000 sq. ft. **Rainforest Pyramid**, a habitat for thousands of exotic plants, tropical birds, butterflies, and fish and characterized by waterfalls, cliffs, caverns, wetlands, and forests. The pyramid also holds a Bat Cave, a 250 sq. ft. completely enclosed habitat, not only the largest of its kind in the Southwest but also the home of several species of Old and New World fruit bats. There is also a Butterfly Hatching Hut where you can watch as butterflies emerge from their chrysalises and flutter into the Pyramid for the first time. Sitting on perches, gold and blue macaws inspect spectators who marvel at their beauty. In all, the Rainforest Pyramid presents the rain forests of Africa, Asia, and the Americas with more than 1,000 species of plant and animal life. A third pyramid, scheduled for completion in 1999, will house the largest aquarium in the Southwest, a 2-million-gallon facility that will hold four types of sea life with species representing Alaska, the Caribbean, Indo-Pacific and Antarctic Oceans.

Another attraction here is **IMAX 3D Theater** that will keep you jumping out of your seat with an experience so real that images on screen appear touchable. If you happen to be at Moody Gardens at Christmas, be sure to see *The Nutcracker,* the age-old classic story full of richly costumed characters and bigger-than-life sets. If you have never experienced snow, here's the next best thing as the 3D film puts you in the middle of a wintry wonderland. This non-ballet version is absolutely enchanting. If time is short and you must choose between this and the Ridefilm, head for the IMAX 3D Theater.

The **IMAX Ridefilm Theater** features a five-minute sensory experience via an 180-degree wrap-around screen and moving seats. Upon entering, you strap on a seat belt and hold on for an *Asteroid Adventure,* for example, a spectacular ride designed by Star Trek generation scientists. The programs rotate, but whatever the subject, this is a shaky experience not suited for people with motion sickness or back problems. If you've been to DisneyWorld and Universal Studios and ridden their simulators, you'll be a little disappointed with this one. However, for less experienced amusement-park goers, this is a good first ride.

The **Discovery Museum,** composed of hands-on demonstrations of scientific principles, explores what life in space will be like. One of Galveston's newest museums housed in a new glass pyramid adjacent to the existing Rainforest Pyramid at Moody Gardens, the Discovery Museum is a creation of Star Trek scientists. Visitors are greeted by a life-sized moving and talking hologram as they enter this state-of-the-art facility. The specter acquaints them with their unusual surroundings before guests move on to intriguing exhibits that tell the story of space travelers who will live, work, and utilize resources in outer space. These interactive exhibits were created with the help of the NASA's Johnson Space Center mind tank. Based on what NASA experts predict will be reality, the exhibits offer a unique opportunity for you to explore a space station kitchen, track a shuttle mission, and ponder distant galaxies and black holes. You can also climb into a likeness of the X-38, a future NASA space station "lifeboat;" get close to a Mars rock; "morph" your face into an alien; and explore the home of tomorrow's space dwellers.

As for outside Moody Gardens, the white-sanded **Palm Beach** awaits with tropical freshwater lagoons and tumbling waterfalls. Parents may play on the volleyball courts while the kids play in the Yellow Submarine with octopus tentacle slides, a periscope, and water guns.

*Note: If you're looking for a Saturday camp for your kids while you explore Galveston's vast history, consider the Moody Gardens' Explorer's Apprentice Camps that offer children year-round experiences and emphasize a variety of topics revolving around nature and the environment. For further details on these camps, call 800/582-4673, ext. 281.*

## The Colonel Paddlewheeler

**One Hope Blvd., docked at Moody Gardens • 409/740-7797, 713/280-3980 • $$, children 3 and under are free for hourly cruises 12 noon, 1 p.m., 2 p.m., 3 p.m., 4 p.m., 5 p.m. • $$$–$$$$ Friday and Saturday evening cruises 8–10 p.m.**

Thanks to the Moody Foundation, Galveston Island now has its own rendition of a romantic 1800s riverboat, in keeping with those who graced the Mississippi during Mark Twain's day. The Colonel, a 325-ton diesel-powered, 800-passenger paddlewheeler, cruises Offatt's Bayou. The captain narrates day cruises, and the evening dinner cruise offers a dance band.

The 152-foot-long *Colonel*, wasn't the first paddlewheeler to the Island. In the glory days before the Great Storm of 1900 when seaport tonnage was at its height, these romantic vessels, with their triple decks and Victorian ornaments, were common along Galveston shores. This 20th century rendition, patterned after the early ones, was named after Colonel William Lewis Moody, a soldier, patriot, statesman, and business leader of the 19th century. A Confederate veteran who spent time as a prisoner of war, he was finally exchanged only to receive serious battle wounds at the siege of Jackson, Mississippi. After many months of critical illness, Moody was pronounced too ill for service and returned to the Island to establish himself as a cotton king. Taking a lead role during the state's difficult post-Reconstruction period, the colonel was instrumental in the founding of the Gulf, Colorado, and Santa Fe railroads and helped reestablish Galveston as an economically successful city before his death in 1920 when he was 92-years-old.

As for his namesake, this romantic paddlewheeler is a favorite of all who buy passage. Her viewing windows and open-air promenade with a top deck and wrought iron furnishings give passengers a gull's eye view of the Bayou that borders the scenic Moody Gardens. Arrive 30 minutes early to ensure yourself a good seat on the open-air upstairs promenade deck. Otherwise, you'll have to sit inside. The paddlewheeler has two main dining salons, "The Galveston Room" and "The Texas Room," along with three bars and three bandstands with two hardwood dance floors. Food during day cruises is limited to the hot dog variety, so if you're health-minded, you may want to eat ashore. The evening cruise provides dinner of a continental nature along with the Dixieland dance band.

## The Lone Star Flight Museum

**2002 Terminal Dr. • 409/740-7722 • Daily 10 a.m.–5 p.m. • Adults $6; children to 13, $3; children under 4, free • Group rates available**

Home of the Texas Aviation Hall of Fame, the Lone Star Flight Museum is one of the finest collections of restored aircraft and aviation exhibits in the nation. Located at Scholes Field in a 72,000-sq.-ft hanger/museum, this display encompasses over 40 vintage aircraft, most in working condition and all reminiscent of "flights of yesterday." This unique collection was not only assembled in honor of the airplane, it is also dedicated to the men and women who flew them in the defense of freedom throughout the world.

Among the collection are WWII fighters, liaison trainers, and executive planes, and bombers. There is also a F7F U.S. Navy Tigercat night fighter here (restored by six persons working full-time for three years) which is one of six Tigercats that still flies. Among the wings is also a twin-fuselage P-38, painted to resemble a fighter flown by WWII ace C. H. "Mac" MacDonald. Named *Putt Putt Maru*, it sports Japanese battle flags painted on the side of the cockpit representing the 27 planes MacDonald shot down. One showy aircraft, the Japanese Mitsubishi A6M2, called the Type 21 "Zero," has made Hollywood appearances in the movies, *Tora, Tora, Tora; Baa, Baa Black Sheep; Black Sheep Squadron; Final Countdown;* and *Midway.* The plane's number is VI-07, the same as the plane flown by Japanese ace Saburo Sakai at Lae and at Rabaul in 1942. He wrote his name on the tail and in Japanese characters his squadron's slogan: "Never Give Up." Other aircraft include the FG-1D Corsair, an AT-6, T28C, and TBM Avenger.

The non-profit museum is manned by volunteers, many of which are pilots or crew members. A tribute to the evolution of aviation, the museum also displays memorabilia, photographs and graphics, a collection of German jet engines, and most important, provides a hands-on experience for members who act as tour guides, artisans, mechanics, machinists, restoration craftsmen, press, photography, display preparation, clerical assistance, receptionists, and speakers.

As soon as you enter the museum, also the custodian of the Eighth Air Force 303rd Bomb Group Memorial, look up. In the entryway, you'll see a comic rendition of homemade efforts to fly in a pedal-driven contraption. The museum is next to Moody Gardens and the Galveston Municipal Airport.

# The Ocean Star
## Offshore Energy Center
Pier 19 • 713/975-6442, 409/766-STAR • Summer hours,
daily 10 a.m.–5:30 p.m. • Winter hours, daily 10 a.m.–4 p.m.
$; children under 7 free • Call for rates on tours

*The Ocean Star,* sponsored by the Offshore Energy Center and located at
the port adjacent to the Mosquito Shrimp Fleet, is an actual offshore rig
designed to give visitors a firsthand feel of oil and gas drilling. The unusual
platform museum gives visitors a true education through interactive displays featuring offshore locations all over the world, videos, and a scale
model of an oil field.

Supported by Exxon and Shell and individuals interested in the "oil
patch," the museum is manned by those in the know who have worked in
the industry, either in the fields or in corporate offices. The center
includes a small Tropical Fish Aquarium Exhibit, providing a view of an
offshore rig from the ocean floor and a ten-minute video on the history of
offshore drilling. There is also a Conference Room, the Ocean Star Theater, a Level 3 Reception Area, all available for corporate events. Closed
Thanksgiving and Christmas.

# The Bolivar Ferry
Ferry Road (State Highway 87) • P.O. Box 381, Galveston 77553-
0381 • 409/763-2386 • Admission free

What better way to smell the salt air than to take an 18-minute ferry
ride across Galveston's harbor 2.7 miles to Port Bolivar, the mainland's
longest peninsula. As a guest of the Texas Department of Highways and
Public Transportation, you get a great view of the harbor, passing tankers
and leisure craft, Seawolf Park, and local wildlife.

As scores of seagulls always fly around the ferry as it glides across the
ocean, you should bring stale bread to feed the flocks. Be sure, however, to
stand at the boat's stern with the wind at your back before feeding them.
Too many birds at the bow block the captain's view, and you'll run the risk
of soiling your summer whites!

All ferries have observation decks, usually crowded with passengers who
leave their cars below deck to get a panoramic view of Galveston Bay. If
you have a keen eye, you might spot a dolphin or two as they playfully
race with the vessels.

The Bolivar Ferry is located on the east end of the island on 2nd St. Six
ferries run every 20 minutes during the day, but at night it runs at specific
hours only. Summer weekends, particularly holiday ones, make for a long
wait. However, you can park your car and board the ferry on foot. To
explore the sparcely-inhabited Bolivar Peninsula, you'll need your car to
drive down Hwy. 87. There you'll see the **Port Bolivar Lighthouse** on the
left. (*See Bolivar Peninsula section for description.*)

## Seawolf Park

Pelican Island • 2106 Seawall Blvd. • 409/744-5738 • $2 adults,
$1 seniors and children

Named in honor of the *USS Seawolf*, a Naval submarine that sank 27
enemy ships and damaged 13, Seawolf Park began with a proposal by the
U.S. Submarine Veterans of WWII to honor the 3,505 submariners lost during that war. Located on Pelican Island and accessed via the 51st St. bridge,
the park is located on the former site of Galveston's immigration station.

When you visit here, explore the *USS Cavalla*, a WWII submarine, and
the *USS Stewart*, a destroyer escort, as well as an M23 Tank and the QF-
86H fighter bomber. Dubbed the "Luckiest Ship in the Submarine Service"
during WWII, the *Cavalla* sank 34,180 tons of Japanese ships, including a
loaded aircraft carrier that participated in the attack on Pearl Harbor.

The *Stewart* was scuttled and captured during the war by the Japanese
who refloated it and re-outfitted it for active duty. By the end of WWII,
the persistent rumor of an enemy ship "that looks like one of ours" was
proven to be true when the U.S. Navy discovered the *USS Stewart* in Japan
after the war.

You are free to board the vessels. That means climbing ladders, elbow-
ing through hatches, and making your way through tight quarters. Wear
tennis shoes, and in the summer, dress in lightweight clothing. As for
meals, plan to picnic on Pelican Island where seagulls fly overhead and an
occasional dolphin raises its head to see what you're having for lunch.
Tables and benches are provided, and there is also playground equipment
for the kids. If you want to fish or crab, you can use the public pier that
takes you out into deeper water. Speckled trout, flounder, and sometimes
red fish make their homes around the end of this pier, so bring your gear.
However, if you didn't pack it, there's a bait camp at the beginning of the
pier that rents rods and reels and sells bait and ice. This attraction offers a
seagull's eye view of the harbor as well.

Bring mosquito repellent in case the wind blows the wrong way and
brings swarms inland.

## Treasure Island Tour Train

21st and Seawall Blvd. • 409/765-9564 • May–Aug.: 9 a.m., 11 a.m.,
1:30 p.m., 3:30 p.m., 5:30 p.m. • Sept.–Nov.: 11 a.m., 1:30 p.m.,
weather permitting. Closed Mondays • Dec.–April: Saturdays only
$—Purchase tickets from the driver

A good way to acclimate yourself to Galveston Island is to take a train
or trolley tour, which boards passengers across from the Hotel Galvez at
the Convention and Visitors Bureau in Moody Center. If the open-air 64-
passenger tourist train is to your liking, you'll find yourself traveling at 15
mph and covering 17 miles around the Island in about 1½ hours. Along the
way, you'll see both the historic and the modern city, including Seawall
Blvd., the business district, historic homes, the Yacht Basin, remains of
Fort Crockett, Rosenberg Library, churches, the Mosquito shrimping fleet,

docks, Jean Lafitte's home, Moody Mansion, Bishop's Palace, Ashton Villa, Downtown Strand, the University of Texas Medical Branch, and other places of interest in between. You'll hear facts about Galveston's early days, including the tragic 1900 Storm, and the city's illegal gambling days. If you have older kids, this is the best choice. Families with smaller children should take a shorter trolley tour. Little ones love to hear the conductor ring the authentic trolley bell. Board at Moody Center, Seawall Blvd. and 21st St. Special group tours available. The Treasure Island Tour Train is the oldest of its kind in Galveston.

## The Galveston Island Trolley

The Strand Visitors Center • 2016 Strand or 2100 Seawall Blvd.
409/765-6655 • Two trolleys run from the Seawall to the Strand
Historic District • Runs every thirty minutes • M–F 6:45 a.m.–7 p.m.,
Weekends 8:45 a.m.–6:15 p.m. • Major Stops: the Visitors Center at
Moody Center on Seawall (across from Hotel Galvez) and Strand
Visitors Center; trolley stops are frequent • 60 cents; transfers are free

The Galveston Island Trolley, hand-built replicas of a late 1800 American trolley that ran on the island from before the turn of the century to 1938, runs a continuous fixed-rail circuit between 21st and Seawall Blvd. to the Railroad Museum along the Strand and Pier 21 and along the beach. This trip also includes a historic commentary, but it's abbreviated. Kids particularly love the experience because they are allowed to stand at the back of the trolley outside the cab and wave at those they pass. Along the way you'll see beautiful historic homes and other points of interest along the route. Another trolley runs throughout the downtown area.

## Air Tours of Galveston Island

2115 Terminal Dr. (Scholes Field main Terminal, Galveston's Municipal Airport) • 409/740-IFLY • Day and sunset tours $$$$

This tour offers 30–40 minute aerial tours of the island, including a run down the beach to the ship channel, a flight over the city's downtown and historic neighborhoods, and a jaunt on to Bolivar Peninsula. The return trips flies over the University of Texas Medical Branch and Pelican Island as well as the Bishop's Palace, Sacred Heart Church, downtown Galveston, Galveston Bay, and the causeway bridge. As the pilot circles to land at the airport, passengers get a fantastic view of Moody Gardens, the Pyramid, and *The Colonel* Paddlewheeler.

## Amaz'N Texas

327 Seawall Blvd. • 409/765-7020 • $; four and younger free • Group rates available

You can try to beat the clock by running through a giant human maze, a wild and crazy two-level labyrinth of twists and turns. If you're weary-of-heart, however, there is a large second-story observation deck to preview the maze prior to entering. Non-maze runners will enjoy observing and filming family and friends who decide to enter as well as take in the breathtaking view from this perch.

## Colonel Bubbie's

**2202 Strand • 409/762-7397**

Whether you like shopping or not, you must visit Colonel Bubbie's, a military surplus store *extraordinaire*. You'll have to see this to believe it because from ceiling to floor this place is filled with WWII tableware and bomb releases that double as light switches, Korean War vintage K-rations, WWI wooden skis, U.S. pilot helmets, submarine parascopes, medals from every country and from the Civil War to Desert Storm, and even rolls of field toilet paper. Open seven days a week, this is a haven for military buffs, junk dealers, avid shoppers, and movie people looking for authentic props.

## The Strand National Landmark Historic District

**20th to 25th streets • 409/763-7080 • The Strand Visitor's Center (Galveston Historical Foundation) • 2016 Strand • 409/765-7834**

This famed historical district, once known as the "Wall Street of the Southwest," is comprised of a host of unique gift and antique stores, restaurants, breweries, galleries, restaurants, museums, and outlet shops. This is the site of the annual Dickens on the Strand festival and Mardi Gras festivities. (*For more on The Strand and its history, see the Strand section.*)

## East End Historic District

**Between Market St. and Broadway from 11th to 19th streets
409/763-5928**

Tree-lined streets in this 40-block sector provide shady havens for some of Galveston's most beautiful residences. All reminders of the "Gilded Age," homes here reflect many architectural examples of Greek Revival Period. Most have been restored and their ornate carvings, stained glass, wraparound porches, and wrought iron fences have been saved. The best way to enjoy the East End Historic District is to walk or take a carriage ride down its quaint streets that are near Galveston's business district, the University of Texas Medical Branch, and the historic Strand District. Governed by the East End Historical District Association, the district has occasional block parties, May Day celebrations, Christmas caroling, and Halloween parties. Carriage rides range from $10 for 15 minutes to $40 for an hour. Arrangements can be made to pick up guests at restaurants, area hotels, or bed and breakfast inns. Some hotels have packages which include this amenity. Among the one-, two- and three-story homes are the Bishop's Palace at 1402 Broadway, The Trube Castle at 1627 Sealy, a Gothic and Moorish structure built by John Clement Trube in 1890, and the majestic Sonnentheil House at 1826 Sealy, a Gothic masterpiece complete with unique balustrades and numerous woodworking details designed by Nicholas J. Clayton. The East End Historical District Association publishes a map of this National Historic Landmark. Call or write the association for a copy. **A Victorian Christmas Home Tour** (Friday evening before Dickens) hosted by the East End Historic District, offers tours of beautifully decorated (in Victorian holiday style) private historical residences as visitors are taken from home to home by horse-drawn carriage. Christmas carolers add to the spirit. Buy tickets *early* (very limited number!) at The Grand 1894 Opera House 409/765-1894.

## Silk Stocking Historic District

**Along 24th and 25th streets from Ave. L to Ave. P ½ • 409/765-7834**

The Silk Stocking Historic District is another of Galveston Island's historic districts that features many fine homes. This is a good place to drive or take a carriage ride through this beautiful old neighborhood.

See Strand Visitors Center, the Galveston Island Convention and Visitors Bureau, and Ashton Villa for brochures on the homes of interest. It was named for a time when only the wealthy ladies could afford silk stockings.

## Garten Verein

**Ave. O and Ursuline at 27th St. • 409/766-2138**

A well-maintained, recently renovated park and pavilion, created by German immigrants in the late 19th century, Garten Verein was a summer place where Germans came to listen to music, socialize, and share meals. Recently preserved by the Galveston Historical Foundation, it is a stunning example of German craftsmanship.

## Galveston Harbour Tours

**Pier 22, berthed behind Fisherman's Wharf and west of the Tall Ship Elissa • Summer: Wed-Sun, hourly tours noon–6 p.m. • Winter: Sat.–Sun., hourly tours noon–3 p.m. • 409/765-1700 • *The Seagull*, P.O. Box 22010, Galveston, TX 77553 (mailing address) • $$**

The Galveston Harbor tour provides a 45-minute narrated boat tour of the oldest seaport in Texas. Guests get a close-up view, seldom enjoyed by the casual visitor, of the sugar, banana, cotton, and sulfur docks; the Grain Elevator; and the "Mosquito Fleet" shrimping boats along the Wharf. Other points of interest include the Tall Ship *Elissa* and the Texas Seaport Museum; Texas A&M University at Galveston; and the University of Texas Medical Branch. One of the best things about this tour is that along the route, dolphins often swim alongside the boat, a 55-foot pontoon, *The Seagull II*. A weekly dolphin watch tour as well as periodic nature excursions are also available. Special tours include the Nature Tours, a fascinating study of the wildlife in and beyond the harbor; Wildlife & Wetlands Excursions, a look at the exotic avian wildlife from the *Seagull II*, a shallow draft vessel, perfect for observation; educational tours, accredited by the Texas Education Agency for grades K–12; and the Pelican Island Circuit, a two-hour circumnavigation of Pelican Island.

The tour guide tells of the port's history sprinkled with tall tales, harbor trivia and anecdotes about pirate ships, paddlewheelers, carpetbaggers, hurricanes, and yellow fever. Along the way, you'll see sugar, banana, cotton, and sulfur docks, grain elevators; rail and barge terminals, tankers and barges; and ships at Galveston shipyards. And ever-present is the seagull that follows its namesake along with great herons and other shorebirds.

*The Seagull II* also offers sundown cocktail and dinner cruises as well as receptions and birthday parties. It also has a flexible itinerary for special catering and group events. Accommodates up to 40 persons.

## Kemp's Ridley Sea Turtle Research Center
## National Oceanic and Atmospheric Administration
## Sea Turtle Research and Rehabilitation Center

4700 Ave. U • 409/766-3523 • By appointment only for groups
If 10 or less, no appointment necessary • 10 a.m., 11 a.m., 1 a.m.,
2 p.m. • Tues.-Sat.; closed Sun., Mon. • Free

Began in 1978, Kemp's Ridley Sea Turtle Research Center is operated by the U.S. Department of Commerce and National Marine Fisheries Service. Its purpose was to establish a laboratory at Galveston to raise, rehabilitate, and maintain endangered sea turtles in captivity for research and for tagging turtles before they are released into the Gulf. At this facility, tanks hold ridleys and loggerheads, all of different ages and sizes. You'll also see sea turtles in sick bay and learn about turtle excluder devices (TEDs), special nets that all shrimpers are required to use.

The building that houses the lab is a little difficult to find. Travel toward the beach on Avenue U and a block off the Seawall, look to your left. There's a trailer house with a blue prefabricated building where the lab is housed in the back.

## Queen Laura's Bordello

2528 Post Office St. • (409) 765-1700 • Group tours available for 15 or more people • $6 a person

Just when you think the big city and its environs hold no more surprises, along comes the opening of a former brothel for family tours and mah-jongg games. Queen Laura's built by a madam in 1886, has undergone few structural changes. The beds and vanities in the bedrooms are original; the hardwood floors are authentic. The parlor features plush velvet sofas and silk lamps with gaudy fringed antiques gathered from local shops but reminiscent of the period. A voluptuous mural by Galveston artist Cara Moore re-creates scenes of an old bordello. And there's a bar and card table where clients gulped whiskey, played poker, and watched the night's entertainment sashay through the room in ritzy evening gowns. Oddly enough, today, the public can rent the former brothel for about $300 to $400 a night; yesteryear's den of sin is the scene for polite luncheons and chic wine and brie benefits. Group tours only.

# Rosenberg Library

2310 Sealy (23rd and Sealy) • 409/763-8854, Fax 763-1064
Mon.–Thurs.: 9 a.m.–9 p.m. • Fri.–Sat.: 9 a.m.–6 p.m. • Sun.,
Sept.–May: 1 p.m.–5 p.m. • Galveston and Texas History Center
(located within the library) • 9 a.m. -5 p.m. Mon.–Sat. • Closed Sun.,
Christmas, most national holidays, and San Jacinto Day • Automated
catalog from home computers: 762-5667 or 5668 • Tours available

The first public library chartered in Texas was the Galveston Mercantile Library founded in 1870, renamed the Galveston Public Library at the turn of the century. Galveston industrialist Henry Rosenberg (1824-93) donated funds by bequest to the Rosenberg Library Association, chartered by Texas in 1900, to give free library service to all Galvestonians. Officially opened in 1904 and recognized as Texas's first public library, the facility is an Italian Renaissance style designed by St. Louis architects Eames and Young. A year later it absorbed the collections of the Galveston Public Library, thus formalizing its role as the public library for the City of Galveston. Known in early days as the cultural center of the community, the library offers historical exhibits, artifacts, architectural drawings from such noted architects as Nicholas J. Clayton, century-old newspapers, maps, photographs, oral histories, artwork, and archives relating to early Texas history and a complete library collection and services. The Moody Wing of the Rosenberg Library, opened in 1971, more than doubled the space of the original structure. Meeting rooms accommodate lectures, recitals, performances, meetings, and other events each year.

The library, headquarters for the Galveston County Library System, serves the general reading public. Another whole dimension, however, can be found on the library's third floor which houses the Galveston and Texas History Center and the Fox Rare Book Room.

The Galveston and Texas History Center collects, preserves, and makes available to the public historic records of Galveston and early Texas. Holdings include manuscripts, photographs, maps, architectural drawings, oral histories, newspapers, pamphlets, and an extensive book collection of Texana. As an important repository of early Texas documents, the History Center provides individual assistance to local historians, scholars, genealogists, and students. The Fox Rare Book Room contains books on the history of printing, fine press editions with particular emphasis placed upon Texas presses, and rare books printed before 1820. Other notables include the papers of Texans Samuel May Williams; Stephen F. Austin; James Morgan, commandant of Galveston Island in 1836; David G. Burnet, first president of the Republic of Texas; Gail Borden, inventor; and H. Kempner, commission merchant and banker.

The Museum Department maintains and exhibits artifacts that document the history of Galveston and early Texas, as well as the Library's fine arts collection. Permanent and temporary exhibits are located on the third floor in the Lykes, Hutchings, and Harris galleries. When at the Rosenberg Library, be sure to check out the watercolors of Galveston artist Boyer Gonzales, known for his scenes that range from the South Texas coastline and landscapes of interior Mexico to those of the New England coast. The grandson of a Spanish army surgeon and offspring of Thomas Gonzales, a prosperous cotton merchant, Gonzales was born into one of Galveston's wealthiest families. Before his death during the Depression, Gonzales became a member of a number of prestigious art societies, including the New York Water Color Society.

## The SEE-Wall Mural

**From 27th to 61st streets and Seawall Blvd.**

The world's longest mural, this SEE-Wall art spans a length of 14,760 feet. Created by 14,000 volunteers and 8,500 area school children and designed by local artists Peter Davis, Mike Janota, and Jane Young, the scenes depict real marine life, birds, and things around Galveston. To view the mural of fish, you have to stand on the beach.

## Jean Lafitte Marker

**1417 Water St. (Ave. A)**

This historical plaque marks the site of Maison Rouge (Red House), the residence of the notorious pirate, Jean Lafitte, who settled for a while in Galveston in 1817 when it was just an encampment. Under the Mexican flag, he and his buccaneers continued forays against Spanish shipping in the Gulf. Maison Rouge was part of Lafitte's fort with its upper story pierced for a canon. The home was luxuriously furnished with booty from captured ships. Leaving the Island in 1821 at the demand of the United States government, Lafitte burned his home, fort, and the entire village. He then sailed to the Yucatan Peninsula.

## Burial Site of David G. Burnet (1788–1870)

**Provisional President of Texas (Mar. 16, 1836–Oct. 22, 1836) • Lake View Cemetery, on 57th St. between Ave. S and Seawall Blvd.**

A statesman who carried a gun in one pocket and a Bible in the other, Burnet acted as a cohesive force in the early days of Texas independence. His dour, quick-tempered disposition, however, kept him from ever gaining wide popularity. As a youth, he took part in the Miranda expeditions (1806,1808) to free Venezuela from Spain, almost losing his life to yellow fever.

## Mosquito Fleet

**Pier 19**

The Mosquito Fleet is comprised of about 200 vessels, including shrimp boats, tugs, party boats, commercial fishing boats, and sightseeing craft. About one-quarter of the fleet is located at Pier 19 near the Ocean Star Energy Museum with the remaining boats docked at Grasso Basin in the

East End behind the University of Texas Medical Branch. The remaining few are scattered around the island. Galveston is one of the oldest shrimp ports in the country existing for more than a century.

During shrimp season, you can see more than 100 trawlers docked at Piers 19 and 20, behind Hill's Pier 19 Restaurant. If you time your visit correctly, you may be able to purchase fresh shrimp and fish directly off the boats. To purchase seafood wholesale and retail, head for the Galveston Shrimp Co., 1902 Wharf, Pier 19. 409/762-1145.

## Texas Heroes Monument

**Broadway & Rosenberg (25th St.)**

Located on Broadway in the center of the esplanade, this 72-foot monument heralds the bravery of the heroes of the Texas Revolution. Designed by Louis Amaties, the highlight of the stoned tribute is the top, a bronze statue of Victory, which extends a laurel wreath toward the site of the Battle of San Jacinto. The monument was a gift to the city from Banker Henry Rosenberg. In 1904, he also gave the city its first library, The Rosenberg Library, known for its wide collection of books, historical documents, and photos.

## The University of Texas Medical Branch Tours

**301 University • 409/772-2618**

Galveston's biggest employer is the University of Texas Medical Branch, which includes four schools and seven hospitals. Nicknamed "Old Red," the Ashbel Smith Building is the highlight of the UTMB tour. Majestic with its red sandstone exterior, it was erected in 1889 by the noted architect Nicholas Clayton. The Ashbel Smith Building is a survivor of the Great Storm and was once the site of the Texas Medical College. Free tours of the center, located on the east side of the island, are available to groups of five or more. Call for reservations.

## Galveston Island Duck Tours

**2411 Strand & corner of 21st St. (Moody Avenue) & Seawall Blvd (Moody Civic Center) • 409/621-4771**

New on the Galveston scene is a small army of "ducks," amphibious vehicles that carry tourists on and off shore for a humorous narrative that lasts approximately 1 hour and 15 minutes. These land and water transports are a great way to not only see island attractions but also provide a creative twist to touring by taking to Offatt's Bayou as well. These "ducks," designed for use during World War II, can be boarded at Moody Civic Center or in the Strand and operate seven days a week at 9 a.m., 11 a.m., 12:30 p.m., 2 p.m., 4 p.m., 6 p.m., and 8 p.m. Call for reservations and be sure to arrive at least 15 minutes before take-off or your seat will go to another excited visitor.

# Sports and Outdoor Recreation

## Golf

### Galveston Island Municipal Golf Course

1700 Sydnor Ln. • 409/744-2366 • Open daily • Green fee rates: under $20 weekdays; under $25 weekends • Tournaments welcome Tournament charges: $3 afternoons and $5 mornings

The municipal 18-hole championship course, ranked among the top five municipal golf courses by *U.S. News and World Report,* is a public course and the country club is a private club, but it does accept reciprocal privileges. Yearly, it hosts the Texas State Mr. & Mrs. Golf Tournament, the Gulf Coast Intercollegiate Tournament and the H&R Invitational Tournament. Lessons are available at the municipal course, and you can rent clubs. The course also has a driving range, a complete practice facility, a pro shop, and a snack bar.

### Galveston Country Club

Stewart Rd. at Pirates' Cove • Guests: $60 weekdays, $65 weekends, does not include cart • 409/737-2776 • 7 a.m. to dark

## Fishing and Boating

For the angler Galveston Island is considered one of the prime Gulf Coast fishing locations. Remote bays, the jetties, the surf, beachfront piers, and offshore fishing afford plenty of opportunities to bring home that really big one.

Year-round, sportsmen can always find something biting from whiting, sand trout, and croaker to flounder, redfish, red snapper, and speckled trout. From May through September, anglers cast their lines for king and Spanish mackerel, ling, silver king tarpon, jackfish, bluefish, and billfish. During their run, Spanish mackerel, a graceful game fish with burnished sides and silver scales flecked with gold, are plentiful around rock jetties. Bull redfish run in the surf after storms, especially in early fall. They are bottom feeders that like rough, sandy water. After one hurricane in 1964, anglers caught about 3,000 redfish in Island waters.

Galveston Bay, a system of four major bays and a number of minor ones, is the seventh largest estuary and fourth most heavily-fished in the United States. These major bays (Galveston, the largest of inland waters; Trinity; West; and East) give the Island the distinction of being one of the most versatile fishing grounds around, whether you like to surf, fresh-water, deep-sea, bay or pier fish, and seine or crab. Remember, however, that all fisherman between the ages of 17-65 are required to have a Texas fishing license, regardless of state of residence. A special three-day salt-water sport fishing license also is available. Licenses can be obtained at most sporting goods stores, tackle shops, bait camps, as well as at many convenience stores.

You might want to pick up a copy of the *Beach Sun*, a local newspaper, which gives such pertinent information as tidal reports, surf conditions, bait suggestions, sun and moon rise and set times, as well as tips for successful fishing and boating. Sting rays are occasionally seen around piers. Portuguese men-of-war and jellyfish are also plentiful in Gulf waters, and local sharks don't seem to mind humans in the water. You might want to use extra-long fish stringers so that if a shark takes after your catch, he won't get you.

## Beachfront/Pier/Surf Fishing

Anglers can fish free off the rock groins and breakwaters along Seawall for flounder, speckled trout, and sand trout. Some say that from 12th to 61st streets, fishermen have luck with speckled trout while casting off the groins when the water is clear. Three fishing piers include the Flagship Pier at 25th St., the 61st St. Pier at 61st St., which charges a small fee, and the biggest, the Gulf Coast Pier at 91st St. Fishermen must comply with Texas Parks and Wildlife regulations and hold a valid Texas Fishing License, except for seniors, for all kinds of fishing.

**Free fishing piers** include the Seawall at 10th, 17th, 27th, and 29th streets, Washington Park, and Offatts Bayou and 61st St. Commercial **fishing piers** include Seawolf Park, located on Pelican Island (409/744-5738); the Galveston Fishing Pier, 90th and Seawall Blvd. (409/744-2273); and 61st St. Fishing Pier (409/744-8365) at Seawall and 61st St. These piers are open year-round weather permitting. Two other notable piers that give excess to the Lower Galveston Bay are Seawolf Park and the lighted pier on the Texas City Dike.

The coastline stretching from the end of the Seawall to San Luis Pass provides good fishing year-round. Speckled trout, Spanish mackerel (smaller than the king), pompano, jackfish, and bluefish bite in the summer, with whiting, redfish, and black drum biting in the fall and winter. The Bolivar Peninsula in the northeast corner of Galveston County has a number of piers, including Mecom's Pier, Dirty Pelican Pier, and the Bolivar Pier.

If you decide to cast directly into the surf by wading, though, wear light waders or jeans to avoid jellyfish or men-of-war bites.

## The Jetties

The North Jetty extends east out into the Gulf of Mexico from Bolivar Peninsula. The South Jetty is a mile down to the south where it reaches into the sea from the east end of Galveston Island. Constructed by granite boulders, both jetties protect the entrances to the Galveston, Texas City, and Houston ship channels. These popular jetties attract a plethora of game fish and, on sunny weekends, are lined with small boats. Land-loving anglers also find the jetties bountiful as they can walk out into deep water without so much as getting a toe wet. Those waters, especially those located at the end of the North Jetty, are historically good spots for larger catches. Tarpon have been known to take bait at the end of the jetties, particularly in July and August.

The Bolivar Pocket, a triangular-shaped area on the Gulf side of the North Jetty, is a very popular wade fishing area. Again, remember to wear jeans or light waders to avoid jellyfish and Portuguese men-of-war stings that can send one to the hospital.

## Bay Fishing

Inshore and bay fishing is great for trout and redfish. Redfish Reef is the dividing line between the lower and upper Galveston Bays. The Ship Channel traverses here with ship traffic determining some areas as off limits. To determine open locations, check the fishing charts.

For speckled trout, try the lower Galveston Bay, particularly around wells and pipelines, especially from June to early September. According to Fishing Authority A. C. Becker, Jr., "Boat fishermen can get into bonanza action using depth sounders to find shell pads where drilling rigs once stood. These same waters are very good for black drum during the annual run that extends from late February through April."

Becker goes on to say that **Trinity Bay**, on Galveston Bay's east side, is the second largest bay of the estuary. "In fishing circles it is known as the 'feast or famine bay.' When the weather is good, speckled trout and redfish abound here. It becomes 'famine bay' in both extreme drought years and usually wet or flood years. Excessive rain and freshwater runoff from the bay's extensive watershed and the Trinity River often make the bay too 'sweet' for some species of salt-water fish." Specks head to waters that surround jetties when bay waters experience excessive changes in salinity.

If you fish in Trinity Bay, watch for feeding birds. Speckled trout swim underneath tell-tale fowls. Marshes around this bay can be reached by boat, and there are places to wade there among abundant wildlife. Since 1983, Texas has been stocking Trinity Bay with striped bass and fingerlings. **West Bay,** the third largest, is a favorite for many. A 20-mile long bay between West Galveston Island and mainland, it stretches from the I-45 Causeway westward to San Luis Pass, the largest natural pass on the Texas Coast. Because San Luis waters act as a tidal funnel, be warned that currents are very strong here and can pull anglers under before they know it.

Seawolf Park, located in Galveston Bay off Harborside Dr. via Seawolf Pkwy. (51st St.), has its own fishing pier for a $2 daily fishing fee (free for senior citizens) and is clean and very accessible. Bay fishing charters typically cost $250–$300 for a half day or $400–$450 for a full day, including bait and tackle.

**San Luis Pass,** in the West Bay, is stable in salinity because of a constant flow of Gulf of Mexico waters, and is home of many seasonal fish and a watery haven for speckled trout. During warm weather months, migratory species such as tarpon, Spanish mackerel, ling, jackfish, bluefish, and a variety of sharks swim here and in the waters of the western part of West Bay. Wade fisherman, who can drift fish here, land speckled trout and redfish in flats behind San Luis Pass. Seasoned fishermen watch for birds that give away trout locations. Carancahua, ten miles from San Luis Pass, is a prime fishing reef in the bay. On the Galveston Island side, there are numerous marshes with coves and small bayous. Considered the best in the entire Galveston estuary shoreline, this is a favorite among locals. Be very careful here, however. There have been a number of anglers pulled under here as West Bay is notorious for strong currents.

**East Bay** is the smallest of Galveston's bays. Some believe it is the best bay of the upper Texas Coast for redfish and flounder. East Bay, a marsh line wedge-shaped bay everywhere but at its mouth, is characterized by many reefs which are great for boaters or waders.

Man-made **Rollover Pass** is 20 miles down Bolivar Peninsula and connects East Bay with Gulf of Mexico. In the fall, flounder and golden croaker run here. *(See the section on Bolivar Peninsula for more on this location.)*

**Dickinson Bay, Chocolate Bay** and **Jones Lake** are minor bays but are good in the fall and spring for redfish on flood tides. Offatt's Bayou, deep and protected from the wind, is known for its abundance of speckled trout and redfish in the winter. Also in the winter, some speckled trout, flounder and redfish remain in the bay while others wait for spring in warmer waters. According to *The Beach Sun,* a local guide, if you must fish in the bitter cold, ". . . take along a popping cork and set it about three feet up from the end of your line and put on a number eight or six treble hook for use with live shrimp. You can adjust the depth of your cork when you are able to determine how deep the trout are running. Soft plastic lures are an excellent choice this time of year also." Winter currents will move you and your boat so you may want to cover a larger area of the bay. Check with your local bait camp for tips on colors and kinds of lures and baits that have had recent luck.

# Offshore Fishing

Galveston's horizon is dotted with many oil production platforms, far offshore banks, and sunken wrecks, including the Flower Gardens, Stetson Rocks, *V. A. Fogg*, and Buccaneer Field. Red snapper run year-round as do other members of the snapper family. During warmer weather, there are king and Spanish mackerel, tarpon, ling, dolphin, bonito, small members of the tuna family, and billfish. Party and charter boats catering to offshore fishing operate out of Pier 18 on the Galveston wharf, the Galveston Yacht Basin, and Tiki Island.

Offshore overnight trips take you 70–100 miles out to waters frequented by Blue Marlin, some weighing up to 800 pounds, White Marlin (50–60 pounds), tuna (5–250 pounds), and Dorado (5–70 pounds). Offshore group charters (four–six persons) range from $400–$1,200 for an 8-hour day, depending on the boat size. Bluewater overnight trips (over 100 miles out) typically leave at 5 a.m. and return at 7 p.m. the next day or leave at midnight and return at 7 p.m. on the same day.

Fishing, in mid-winter months, is a probable time for catching whiting, black drum, and an occasional redfish.

## Fishing Charters and Party Boats

**A+ Charters**
800/880-7587

**Abra-Cadabra**
713/893-6791

**Aqua Safari Charters**
409/935-4646, 800/759-4547

**Brand X**
409/763-2880

**Painless Sailing Tour**
409/739-9538

**Coastal Yacht Brokers**
409/763-3474

**Extra Labor Charters**
409/765-9700

**Galveston Charter Service**
409/762-8535

**Galveston Party Boats**
409/763-5423

**Good News**
409/765-9191

**T-N-T**
800/482-0074

**Reel Adventures**
409/744-5464

**The Angler**
409/763-3072

**Williams Party Boats**
409/762-8808, 713/223-4853

**Yacht Basins/Marinas**
Boat Launches are located at Teichman Rd., Sportsman Rd., and Washington Park, 61st St.

**Galveston Yacht Basin**
Holiday Dr. & Wharf

**Jamaica Beach Marina**
4002 Bob Smith Dr.

**Payco Marina**
8821 Broadway

**Sea Isle Marina**
21706 Burnett Dr.

**Pirates' Beach Marina**
14302 Stewart

**T-Marina**
Offatts Bayou at 61st

# OTHER OUTDOOR RECREATION

## Surfing

A number of state and Gulf Coast surfing championships are held on Galveston Island. Exclusive surfing areas and "no surfing" areas are designated. Boards may be rented from the numerous concessions along the beach.

## Scuba Diving

Several good spots are near offshore oil rigs from one to fifty miles south of Galveston. For information, contact any of the local dive shops listed in the phone book. Flower Gardens, a live coral reef, is 110 miles offshore.

## Net Sports

Volleyball courts are at **East Beach (R.A. Apffel Park)**, **Stewart Beach Park**, **Seawolf Park**, and **Dellanera RV Park**. Racquetball and tennis courts are available at the **Galveston Health and Racquet Club**, 83rd and Airport (409/744-3651).

## Waterslides

There are two waterslides on the Island, **Jungle Surf Water Slide**, 9402 Seawall Blvd.(at 94th and Seawall Blvd), and **Stewart Beach Water Coaster**, located at the intersection of Broadway and Seawall Blvd. Both slides operate seasonally. Jungle Surf (409/744-4737), Watercoaster (409/762-6022).

## Horseback Riding

Enjoy horseback riding on the beach at **Sunshine Stables**, 11118 West Beach, and **Gulf Stream Stables**, 8 Mile Rd., West Beach. Sunshine Stables (409/744-7470), Gulf Stream (409/744-1004).

## Miniature Golf Courses

There are two miniature golf courses on Galveston Island. **Magic Carpet Golf**, 9030 Seawall (409/740-2000), at 90th and Seawall Blvd., is an 18-hole miniature golf course with animation, waterfalls, and tropical landscapes, a giant flower, and a windmill and pendulum. Get your ball past the Texas Fire Ant, Serpent, Spider, and Alligator. Play aboard the Pirate Ship or high atop a castle. Open year-round weather permitting. Also has nine-stall batting cages from baseball-slow to baseball-fast and slow-pitch softball. Hourly batting cage rental is available through advance reservation. Snow cones, soft drinks, and picnic tables also available. Special rates offered for groups of 20 or more with advance notice. The course is located across from the Galveston Fishing Pier on the Gulf of Mexico.

**Stewart Beach Miniature Golf**, 401 Seawall Blvd., is located at Broadway and Seawall Blvd. (409/762-3935).

## Bumper Boats

**Stewart Beach Park** • **409/765-5023**

## Kite Flying

Tropical wind blows at a steady rate sending kites billowing while breakers rhythmically crash below every six seconds.

To purchase a colorful kite, visit Kites Unlimited, Seawall Blvd. and 99th, 409/744-4121,

# Bird Watching

### Great Texas Birding Classic (1-888-TX-BIRDS)

Fifty-three species of seagulls call Galveston Island home. Laughing gulls command attention with a wing span almost a yard long, and a fanatical laugh that resembles that of a human. The Franklin gull, blackheaded with wing tips to match; the herring gull; and the skimmer gulls all dive for fish and follow the ferries as they make their way across Galveston Bay.

# Sea Shell Hunting

Walkers and runners enjoy combing the 32-mile long beach for sand dollars, clams, scallops, whelks, tulips, and wentletraps.

# THE STRAND HISTORIC LANDMARK DISTRICT

## Strand Visitors Center

2016 Strand • Galveston, TX 77550 • 409/765-7834, 713/280-3907
www.galvestonhistory.org.

The Strand Visitors Center has what you need to get the most out of your visit to The Strand Historic Landmark District including brochures, maps, tour information, ticket sales, an orientation film, and even an audio tour that sets visitors loose on the streets with an audio player and cassette that gives the history of significant buildings and this 36-square block area that was once called the "Wall Street of the Southwest."

## HISTORY

The **Strand Historic Landmark District** was formerly the wealthiest commercial center west of the Mississippi. In its heyday it was the location of the largest and most important wholesale houses west of the Mississippi River from cotton, paint, drug, grocery, hardware, and cotton dealers to dry-good stores and insurance companies. Here at the mouth of Texas' once busiest seaport, sophisticated financial transactions were handled by mercantile firms since chartered banks had not been approved by Congress. Through its fleeting years of success, the Strand became the birthplace for many fortunes, rooted in cotton, finance, and shipping.

All who struck deals here were in "high cotton" until Nature placed an angry hand, in the form of a giant tidal wave, on the flourishing island. When the waters of the Great Storm of 1900 began to subside, buildings within the financial district stood in ruins, and so floated the hopes and dreams of Galveston entrepreneurs. Some rebuilding occurred, but coupled with the Depression, the Strand was gradually transformed into a string of deserted streets full of tales of what might have been.

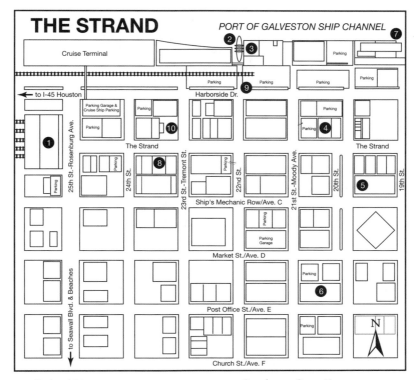

**THE STRAND**

1. Railroad Museum
2. Tall Ship Elissa/Pier 21
3. Texas Seaport Museum
4. Strand Visitors Center
5. David Taylor Classic Car Museum
6. Grand 1894 Opera House
7. Ocean Star Energy Center
8. Mardi Gras Museum
9. Great Storm Museum
10. Saengerfest Park

Today, however, the Strand has experienced a renaissance, alive again because of the Galveston Historical Foundation, which has just celebrated its 125th anniversary, and diehard city supporters who have succeeded in making the Strand a tourist attraction full of more than 100 shops, antique stores, restaurants, and art galleries, all set in architecture unique to this Gulf Coast seaport. Visitors have a number of annual events to choose from such as Dickens on the Strand that always occurs the first weekend in December to the island's annual Mardi Gras extravaganza in February. But even if a tourist is not present during an official event, they have a wide choice of places to visit. They may decide to walk the decks of the foundation's restored 1877 square rigger docked at Pier 21 (off Harborside Dr.) and see its companion the **Texas Seaport Museum**, which highlights the workings of the 19th century port and its continued influence on the region.

But whether one goes to The Strand to shop, dine, or just soak in a little Texas history, all will agree that this 36-square block area is worth seeing. Over 90 shops, antique stores, galleries, and restaurants surround museums and the queen of the port—the 1877 Tall Ship Elissa.

## Mode of Transportation within the Strand

Located on the north side of the Island, a block off the port, the restored district can be found primarily between 20th and 25th (Rosenberg) Streets. Parking is available throughout the district, or you can catch a trolley and get off at the Strand and 21st streets. This will put you only a few steps from The Strand Visitors Center, 2016 Strand (409/765-7834) (in Houston 281/280-3907) open daily 9:30 a.m.–5 p.m. Manned by the historical foundation in the old 1859 Hendley Building, employees answer questions and offer maps of The Strand. You can also buy tickets for many of the visitor attractions. Once you arrive, walking is recommended, or you may decide to take a horse-drawn buggy.

The Galveston Historical Foundation staff members can assist in planning pre-arranged group tours (minimum 20 persons) and educational tours for student groups. With 24-hours advance notice, trained guides are available to conduct walking tours of The Strand and driving tours of historic Galveston Island for pre-arranged groups.

# THE STRAND'S HISTORIC BUILDINGS

Your starting point will be the Visitors Center, housed in the historic **Hendley Building,** which during the Civil War was used alternately by both Union and Confederate forces as headquarters as control of the city passed back and forth between them. As you make your way along the quaint streets, note the **1871 League Building** on The Strand at Tremont, which houses several shops as well as the classy Wentletrap Restaurant. Also look for the **Marx and Kempner Building,** 2100 block of the Strand, to see how artisans hand-painted a trompe l'oeil mural, an image that resembles the original ornate facades lost when the original detailing of the building was removed many years ago. The **1882 H.M. Trueheart-Adriance Building,** 210 Kempner, also deserves your notice as it was designed by the famous Island architect Nicholas J. Clayton. One of the most impressive structures in the Strand, it was the restoration of this building that sparked the Strand's renaissance. For a second example of Clayton's work, see the **Adoue-Lobit Bank Building,** 2102 Strand, built in 1890 to house the once substantial bank house of Adoue-Lobit, although little of the original ornate design remains except the ground-floor arcade of cast iron columns. Note also the 1895 Hutching Sealy Bank Building, 2326 through 2328 Strand and 24th, also designed by Clayton, which is built in high Victorian style. (*For a detailed description on the 1895 Hutchings Sealy Bank Building, see the section on historic homes and buildings.* To discover additional buildings, refer to the *Galveston Foundation's Walking Guide,* which gives information about the buildings and also acquaints tourists with other Strand sights.)

# The Grand 1894 Opera House

2020 Postoffice • For show information, call 409/765-1894 or
800/821-1894 • Open daily for self-guided tours

*The Grand 1894 Opera House is also the setting for two summer musicals
sponsored and performed by the Lone Star Performing Arts Association, which
offers three venues on the Island annually. Call 800/54-SHOWS for the
association's schedule.*

The Grand 1894 Opera House is a year-round performing arts theater,
magnificently restored in 1986 and designated as "the official Opera
House of the State of Texas by the 73rd legislature." Dubbed as among the
nation's finest historical restorations, the opera house once provided a Gulf
Coast stage for such greats as Lillian Russell, Sarah Bernhardt, the Marx
Brothers, Anna Pavlova, Al Jolson, and John Philip Sousa. More recently,
such entertainers as Gregory Hines, Ben Vereen, and Loretta Swit have
brought scores to the theater which also features world-famous Broadway
musicals.

The history of the opera house began with its grand opening in 1895.
*The Galveston Daily News* article on the opening of the Grand Opera House
described it as ". . . the grandest temple of Thespis to be found in the
broad confines of Texas and the Southwest." In those early days, the
impressive Sullivan-style carved stone arch, the glittering crystal chande-
lier in the sophisticated main lobby, and lighting by electricity and gas
made the house not only impressive but progressive. Created by Galveston
firm Barnes and Palliser under the direction of Frank Cox of New Orleans,
the house is reflective of Cox's innovative ideas, including his elimination
of square corners to implement effective acoustics.

The architect also made sure that seats in the house were no more than
70 feet from the stage. Called the "parquette," the innovative seating plan
arranged the 1,500 seats in a curve and descended downward toward the
stage, giving a clear view from every spot. Seating in the balcony and
gallery was arranged in the same way with the best seats in the house the
first two rows of the balcony. Two sets of box seats on parquette and balcony levels were outfitted with silk, satin, and silver railings. Plush
draperies complimented walls decorated with painted borders of "festoons
of roses looped and knotted with bows and ribbons," and over the stage,
lover's knots, tropical flowers, masks, play books, and other theatrical symbols acted as crown for the stage that was considered the largest in the
state and in the Southwest.

Although no remnants of original curtain remained, old black and white
photos and newspaper accounts describe an opulent painting of the Greek
poet, Sappho, daydreaming in a boat while nymphs on the shore called
her to prepare for a performance in the theater across the lagoon. Earl Sta-
ley, winner of the prestigious Prix de Rome, an artist well-versed in Greek

mythology, designed the new curtain for the Montreal company of Michael Hagen to paint.

In the old days, a production of *Ben Hur* involved a chariot race with one chariot turning on a treadmill as the scenery moved behind it. It was rumored that one of the city's fire-engine horses was used to pull the chariot. There were also early performances of *La Boheme*, *The Wizard of Oz*, *Hedda Gabler*, *Babes in Toyland*, *Il Trovatore*, and *Madame Butterfly*. In addition, old records show that Tex Ritter rode his horse, White Flash, down the aisle and, somehow, onto the stage.

Now a theater with modern, state-of-the-art theatrics, the 1894 Grand Opera House is one of the few remaining theaters of its era in Texas and has earned its place on the National Register of Historic Places. Thanks to the Harris and Eliza Kempner Fund, The Moody Foundation, the Houston Endowment, and gifts from George and Cynthia Mitchell, the $7 million dollar facelift was completed a little over a century after it was built. Today the opera house stands as yet another example of Galveston's persistence to live on.

## The 1877 Tall Ship *Elissa*

**Pier 21, one block off the Strand • Weekdays 10 a.m.-5 p.m. (extended weekend hours) • 409/763-1877, 713/488-5942 $5 adults, $4 students, 6 and under free • Special family packages available • www.phoenix@net-tsm**

The 1877 Tall Ship *Elissa*, Galveston's historic 1877 200-foot-long square-rigger was saved by the Galveston Historical Foundation who found her lifeless and decaying in a Pireaus, Greece scrap yard. The organization purchased her for $40,000, repaired portions of her hull, towed her back to Galveston, a port she twice visited during her heyday, and began a complete restoration.

The *Elissa*, whose main mast towers its deck by over 100 feet, was first launched from a Scottish builder's yard in 1877, a little over a decade after the Civil War. In addition to her trips to Galveston in the 1920s, this iron baroque beauty had also visited such ports-of-call as Calcutta and Tampico. At one point she found herself in the hands of Greek smugglers and eventually lay for many years in the Greek scrap yard minus her sailing rig. That was a long way from Pier 21 where she is today, beautifully restored to her original beauty. Since her rebirth, the *Elissa* has represented Galveston and Texas by sailing to New York for the Statue of Liberty Centennial Celebration. She accompanied the Class A Tall Ships and was the oldest of her class and the only restored 19th-century square-rigger in the parade of sails.

Guests may climb aboard the vessel, located at the end of 23rd Street at Pier 21, stand at the wheel, and go below where there is a display that shows the ship's history.

# The Great Storm Theater

Pier 21 • Harborside Dr. at 21st St., second floor • 409/763-8808
Sun.–Thurs., 11 a.m.–6 p.m. • Fri.–Sat., 11 a.m.–8 p.m. • Adults
$3.50; students (7–18) $2.50, under six free • Discounts for
pre-arranged group tours

This 27-minute award-winning, multi-image account of the 1900 Great
Storm gives visitors a chilling glimpse into the devastating 1900 Storm
that claimed the lives of 6,000 from a population of 40,000 and leveled
Galveston Island. Based on diaries and letters of survivors, the presentation
explains how the storm marked the point in Galveston history, once the
most important seaport in Texas.

Historic photographs, artists' renderings, visual effects, and dramatic
sound enhanced by Dolby 4-track Surround Sound are also added to the
eye-witness accounts. The show, which begins on the hour throughout the
day, brings to life the deadliest natural disaster in United States history,
describes a tidal wave that literally covered the island from Gulf to bay,
and highlights the brave comeback of the islanders who showed determi-
nation and courage to survive.

# Port of Galveston

Port Industrial Blvd. • Along Water St. on the north side of the island
from 9th to 41st

It was through this port that European immigrants entered Galveston in
the 19th century with the hope of finding a new life in Texas. Many
stayed and made enormous fortunes here. Port development began on the
island's east end where the medical center is today. Wharf development
was moved toward 20th St. where the water was deeper. The first cargo
(cotton), to go directly from Galveston to England left here in 1839.

Today, container ships, grain carriers, shrimpers, and banana boats all
use the port, which claims to have the fastest access to the open seas of
any major American port. It also is the only port in America where all
facilities—from railroad switching to crating—are coordinated under one
management.

# Mardi Gras Museum

Old Galveston Square/2211 Strand, third floor • 409/763-1133
Wed.–Sun. 12 a.m. to 6 p.m. • Closed Mon.–Tues. • Adults $2;
students (7–18) $1, under 7 free • Available for rentals

Located in Old Galveston Square, the Mardi Gras Museum is the epito-
me of what the French call "Laissez les bon temps roulé!" ("Let the good
times roll.") In celebration of Galveston's rich carnival traditions, three galleries of flashy carnival exhibits, many dating back to some of the earliest
events of the 19th century, showcase historic costumes, elaborate masks,
glittering crowns and scepters, ball gowns, Treasure Ball capes, invitations,
photographs, models of the street arches created by local artisans, and
other Galveston Mardi Gras memorabilia.

You learn facts about the city's earliest 1867 celebration of Fat Tuesday to those of today. There is also a display here that explains the evolution of the rival krewes who stage the city-wide carnival with dazzling torchlit night parades and fabulous masked balls. Once you've visited this museum, you'll understand the "pomp and circumstance" that makes this yearly carnival a glittery affair. The museum includes a gift shop.

## The Railroad Museum

**Center for Transportation and Commerce • 25th & Strand streets 409/765-5700 • Summer: daily 10 a.m.–4 p.m. except Mardi Gras weekend and major holidays • Winter: closed Mon.–Tues. • Adults $5, seniors $4.50, children (4-12) $2.50 • Free parking in back**

Chug on to the Railroad Museum, and let a lonesome whistle of a distant locomotive take you back to the fading days of train travel. Formally called Center for Transportation and Commerce, this museum houses the largest collection of restored rail cars and locomotives in the Southwest United States. Visitors here may actually board the long rows of Pullman cars, steam locomotives, mail cars, coaches, cabooses, and diners that sit still on tracks located behind the depot. View 20,000 pieces of railroad equipment and memorabilia at this 5½-acre museum.

Another pull here is the working model of the Port of Galveston featuring HO-gauge model miniature trains, pulling cargo to and from Galveston rail terminals. Children can actually crawl under the scale model and poke their hands up into plastic viewing circles, which give them a giant's-eye view of all the activity. Films and exhibits also share Galveston's railroad and commerce history.

The museum's most spectacular attraction, however, is The People's Gallery, based in an authentic Santa Fe Depot Waiting Room. There you'll find 32 stark white plastered "apparitions" who have somehow been caught in a kind of time warp. Frozen sculptures, all created by artists and brothers, Ivan and Elliott Schwartz, are in authentic 1932 clothing. By picking up "hearphones" that accompany every figure, guests can eavesdrop on conversations between ghostly travelers.

Sleep-overs that involve exploration of antique trains are offered for groups of kids.

## The Galveston County Historical Museum

**2219 Market St. • 409/766-2340 • Summer: Mon.–Sat. 10 a.m.–5 p.m., Sun. 5 p.m. • Winter: Mon.–Sat. 10 a.m.–4 p.m., Sun. 12 p.m.–4 p.m. • Free**

A project of the Galveston Historical Foundation and the Galveston Commissioners Court, the Galveston County Historical Museum depicts life from prehistoric times to the present as it existed on the Island, its surrounding mainland, and the Bolivar Peninsula. Marvel at the exquisite beauty of the crystal lens taken from the old South Jetty Lighthouse, and kids can climb on an 1836 cannon from the Navy ship *Brutus*. A. L. Bogotto's General Store, brought in tact from Dickinson, Texas, occupies the first floor. On the second floor, exhibits, each depicting some aspect of Galveston history, change every few weeks.

Once the 1919 City National Bank Building, the museum gives you a chance to learn how lighthouses have protected the Gulf Coast for more than a century. You will also learn about the Akokisa, the first inhabitants of Galveston County and their encounters with the region's earliest European explorers. Permanent exhibits focus on topics such as island architecture and the Great Storm of 1900.

## David Taylor's Classic Car Museum

**1918 Mechanic St. • 409/765-6590 • Mon.–Sat., 10 a.m.–5 p.m. Sun. 12 p.m.– 4 p.m. • $5 adults; $4 children, students, and senior citizens**

Displayed in the typical atmosphere of a car dealership of its 1914 Marshner Building, this museum showcases perfect-condition "luxury cars of the wealthy and hot rods of our youth," dating from the 1920s to the 1960s, all in immaculate running condition. Maintained by local Texan and successful car dealer, the recently-deceased David Taylor has created within the confines of the Strand District a shrine to the auto industry by featuring 53 vintage automobiles that depict an era when big was best.

You'll find the actual 1940 Mercury that movie legend Clark Gable gave to his glamorous wife, actress Carole Lombard. Other favorites include a 1936 Cadillac V-12 Convertible, a 1934 Ford Roadster, a 1927 Buick Roadster, a 1937 Cord Phaeton 812, a 1955 Chevrolet Bel Air Two-Door Sedan in shades of pale pink and gray. Others include a fire-engine red 1931 Packard Super Eight 840 Convertible Coupe, a 1931 Cadillac V-8 Fleetwood Roadster, and a 1940 Lincoln Continental Cabriolet.

## The Ocean Star Museum

**Pier 19 • 713/975-6442 or 409/766-STAR • Summer: daily 10 a.m.–5 p.m. • Winter: daily 10 a.m.–4 p.m. • $5 adults; $4 senior citizens and students**

Sponsored by the Offshore Energy Center, this three-deck museum is actually aboard an offshore rig. Visitors learn how oil and gas are produced offshore. Videos, interactive displays, and models take patrons to offshore locations all over the world.

## Mosquito Fleet

**Pier 19**

Walk to Pier 19 and see the Mosquito Fleet, comprised of about 200 vessels, including shrimp boats, tugs, party boats, commercial fishing boats, and sightseeing craft. About one-quarter of the fleet is located here next to the Ocean Star Energy Museum with the remaining boats docked at Grassobasin in the East End behind the University of Texas Medical Branch and a few others scattered around the island. Galveston is one of the oldest shrimp ports in the country, having existed for more than a century.

## Texas Seaport Museum

**Pier 21 (next to the 1877 Tall Ship Elissa and Harborside Dr. at 21st St.) • 409/763-1877 • Summer: daily 10:30 a.m.–5:30 p.m. • Winter: daily 10 a.m.–5 p.m. • Admission includes self-guided tours of the Texas Seaport Museum and the Elissa, two theater presentations, and access to the immigration database. • $5 Adults; (7–18/seniors (65+) $4 students; under 7 free • Discounts for families and pre-arranged group tours • Available for rentals and children's overnight programs**

The Texas Seaport Museum, located on the dock next to the *Elissa*, highlights the workings of the 19th century port and its role in local and national history. Exhibits tell the story of the cargo and people who went through the Port of Galveston during the 19th century. Visitors also are invited to examine a computer database with information about more than 133,000 immigrants, those who entered the United States through Galveston's port, and their countries of origin, dates of arrival, and planned destinations. Once known as "The Ellis Island of the West," Galveston became home for many who felt they had indeed reached the promised land.

The 1877 Tall Ship *Elissa*, a floating National Historic Landmark, is berthed here a gangplank away so visitors may experience the beauty of the ship firsthand. A stroll of its immaculate decks and a visit below into the vessel's hole to view quarters and exhibits entitled "Life at Sea" and "Sounds of Sea" gives landlovers a true view of life on the high seas over 100 years ago. Learn about the *Elissa*'s rescue from a Greek scrap yard and her costly restoration by the Galveston Historical Foundation. (*For more on the* Elissa, *built in Scotland over 125 years ago, see the Attractions section.*)

## Strand Theater

**2317 Ship's Mechanic Row • 409/763-8659**

Built in the restored 1871 Opperman Building, this is a variety theater offering comedies, a children's series, movies, musicals, magic, dance, readings, classes, and concerts year-round. The theater offers an intimate setting with only 205 seats, which includes balcony seating. For event schedule, call 409/763-4591.

(*To see listings of Strand attractions, museums, and accommodations, see those sections.*)

# Strand Shopping

If you like to shop, The Strand has within walking distance every conceivable shop: outlet stores, antique shops, art galleries, and warehouses packed with military memorabilia. Most of the shops are nested within the historic buildings that once housed a business center known as "The Wall Street of the Southwest."

Wear comfortable shoes, and when it's time to eat, follow the gourmet aromas emanating from one of the many restaurants.

## Strand Antiques

Browsers will discover a host of antique stores such as **Hendley Market,** 2010 Strand (409/762-2610), which specializes in Victorian jewelry and sewing items, beaded bags, early books, and laces. Around the corner, shoppers can taste resident-made peanut butter at the **Peanut Butter Warehouse,** 100 20th St. (409/762-8358) where three floors are filled with antiques, collectibles, and other gift items. The warehouse also has a boutique of vintage clothing that visitors may try on. This is a good place to find something to wear for Dickens-on-the-Strand. **Somewhere in Time,** 124 20th St. (409/762-1094), includes an assortment of collectibles, pottery, toys, and soda memorabilia. For glass, porcelain, and lamps, **Yesterday's Best** at 120 20th St. (409/762-0335) is one sure bet for the serious shopper.

Over at 2212 Mechanic St. the **Serendipity Antiques and Collectibles** (409/763-5799) provides a "one-of-a-kind" shopping experience providing a large variety of antiques, collectibles, home decor, and gifts.

On the next block, **Made in France,** 2309 Mechanic St. (409/762-3327) specializes in French country antiques and unique collectibles. The **Cat's Meow Antique Shop,** 2428 Mechanic St. (409/763-2575), features '50s and '60s modern Texas pine, Victorian antiques, pottery, and unusual items. Shoppers shouldn't pass up **La Maison Rouge,** 418 22nd St. (409/763-0717), where 25 dealers showcase European and American furniture, art, pottery, fine glass, china, estate jewelry, sterling and plate silver, vintage linens, and African and ethnic artifacts. On the next block at 2120 Postoffice, the **Encore Gallery** (409/762-7780) offers a collection of antiques, contemporary art, Persian carpets, Venetian glass beads, and jewelry. **B.J.'s Antiques and !,** 2111 Postoffice (409/763-6075), offers crystal, china, Majolica pottery, jewelry, Dick & Jane readers, and carnival, vaseline glass and granite ware.

## Strand Factory Outlets

Factory outlets include the **Bass Shoe Outlet,** 2313 Harborside (409/765-7199). For furniture and home decorating items, visit **Goodwin Weavers Showroom** at 2228 Strand (409/762-8006). There's also a **Van Heusen Factory Outlet** at 2222 Strand (409/935-6183) and a **Mikasa Factory Outlet,** located at 2225 Strand (409/765-1760), which is a factory store for fine tabletop, house, and gift wares. Browsers can also walk to the corner to find the **New York Dress Outlet,** 2228 Mechanic, (409/762-1916), which has a collection of famous label dresses, and suits at factory prices (sizes 2 to 24).

## Other Strand Shops

For Indian and Southwestern jewelry and art, walk over to the **Santa Fe Trail,** 2311 Strand (409/762-7511).

Within the Old Galveston Square Building that houses the Mardi Gras Museum upstairs, you'll find a number of shops including the **Prestige Fragrance & Cosmetics,** 2211 Strand (409/765-8990), where you can buy an aromatic array of fragrances and cosmetics. The **Tejana Rose,** 2211 Strand (409/762-7008), sells one-of-a-kind fine ladies apparel and accessories. **The Strand Brass and Christmas on The Strand,** 2119 Strand (409/762-7400) is a good place to buy quality brass, imported lace, and also offers Christmas items year-round.

**Surf Styles,** 2410 Strand (409/763-0147), offers beach attire while **Ye Old Market Antiques,** 2408 Strand (409/763-9628), and **Su Casa Southwest Interiors,** 2402 Strand (409/763-2424), are perfect places to find just the right pieces to decorate one's home. On the corner is **Morgan's Fine Ladies Apparel,** 206 24th St. (409/763-3498). Its clientele is the female sophisticate who knows her brand names. One block over on Ship's Mechanic Row, **Monsieur Andre** (409/762-2580) sells designer men's fashions while **Sean Miles** (409/763-7177) helps the ladies with designer fashions. Both shops are located at 2300 Mechanic, in the Tremont House.

Twenty-third St. offers **Something Special** at its home at 2317 Strand (409/762-2473). The **Atrium Boutique** (409/762-4979), **Unexpected Pleasures** for unique gift items, and **Kaleidoscope,** all at 2313 Strand, are great places to find a truly unusual present for that special person. Other shops line that same hall from **Intima Lingerie Boutique** (409/762-7331), **Crabtree & Evelyn, Ltd.** (409/762-6193), **Santa Fe Trail** at 2311 Strand (409/762-7511), and **Save the Planet** at 2309 Strand (409/762-0008). For fine papers and gifts, Jeep Collins jewelry and collectible houses, try **The Curiosity Shoppe,** 2119 Strand, (409/762-4893).

The **Discovery Store,** 2326 Strand (409/765-5755), is perfect for the inquisitive child and nature enthusiast, and **Maggie's,** 2326 Strand (409/762-6816), offers clothing and accessories. For the latest trends in clothing for young people, visit **Flores Soneu** (409/763-5741) and **Jammin' Sportswear,** (409/763-4005), both at 2314 Strand. **Goodbar's Faux Jewelry & Gifts** is at 2301 Strand. The side street, 23rd St. (Tremont), is where tourists find the **Sunglass Hut,** 110 Tremont (409/765-1778), for discounted sunglasses.

You haven't shopped until you've visited **Col. Bubbie's Strand Surplus Center** (409/762-7397) and **The Barracks,** 2202 Strand, which offer surplus military clothing and supplies. The stores are enclosed in a gigantic warehouse and are filled with every kind of military memorabilia imaginable—real ejection seats and Spanish saddle bags. Once you've purchased your WWII pilot's helmet, walk across the street to the **Blue Moon Gold-**

smith (409/762-6662) and **Best Buddies,** a doll shop (409/763-6592), both at 2221 Strand. Of course, you can't leave Galveston without buying a seashell or two. **Island Shells & Souvenirs,** 101 Kempner (409/744-3995), has quite a "sea" of oceanic treasures.

To walk the beaches in style, check out the **Tropicana Outlet** and **Island Fashions,** 2128 Strand (409/763-5539), for just the right swimsuit. **T-Body's & More,** 2124 Strand (409/762-7426), and **Conversation Pieces,** 2114 Strand (409/763-1230), also offer styles that set you apart from the traditional crowd.

If you tire of shopping and begin to feel hunger pangs, stop for a bite at the **Old Strand Emporium,** 2112 Strand (409/763-9445) and have a mug of imported or domestic beer while you're at it. If wine is more suited to your palate, there is an extensive wine cellar here. Before you leave, stroll to the back to see the Wurlitzer Military Band Organ, player pianos, and old-time jukeboxes in the back.

On 21st St. (Moody) stop in at **Bayside Gifts** and **Swischuk's Monograms & Prints** (409/765-8131) all at 101 Moody. Next you'll find **Animal Smackers** (409/762-0490), **Jewelry & Gifts, Cottage Arts, Noah's Ark Arts & Crafts** and **Colonial Rose Quilt Co.** (409/763-4997), all at 104 Moody. Down the street is **Couteux Couture,** 212 Moody (409/763-3363), and **Twinkle Toes,** 210 Moody (409/762-7178).

On the last block of the Strand, 20th St., you'll find **Earth Alert,** 2027 Strand (409/765-9474), for the Earth-conscious shopper and **Sea Sensations,** 2029 Strand (409/763-0060), **Cotton & Gold Factory Outlet** (409/762-7446), and **The Hat People** (409/765-6126), both at 2021 Strand.

## Strand and Gallery Row Galleries

For art in the Strand Historic Landmark District, visit **The "Artist" Loft,** 2326 Strand (second floor of Hutchings-Sealy Building), where the art of local artist Joe Battle is displayed. Nearby is the **J. Bangle Gallery,** 2319 Strand (409/763-6161), where art admirers can choose from original work of local architecture, the Tall Ship *Elissa,* and port scenes. Antiques, art, accents and custom picture framing are also available. **Don Rouse's Wildlife Gallery,** 2314 Strand (409/763-1391), features original art, prints, and sculptures by Texas and nationally known artists. **Two Friends Gallery,** 2301 Strand (409/765-7477), showcases contemporary crafts including clay, fiber, metal and glass, all by American artists. The **Galveston Arts Center,** 2127 Strand (409/763-2403), features the work of emerging and established regional artists in all types of media. At Pier 21 you'll find the **Admiralty Marine Model Gallery** (409/766-1777), which offers museum-quality ship models, nautical art, sculptures and gifts. You'll also find **Pier I Imports,** 2100 Harborside Dr. (409/763-2643). Also on The Strand is **Yaga The Store,** 2111 Strand (409/762-2773), which offers fun men and women's sportswear and trendy accessories.

Four blocks from Galveston's Historic Seawall is the **Galveston Gallery,** 1825 Rosenberg (25th St.) (409/763-6116), which includes the work of

Texas artists in watercolors, oils and canvas, mixed media, sculpture and fiber art in subjective, abstract and contemporary styles. Every six weeks, the art galleries join together to host **ArtWalk,** an evening of openings and receptions of new works by local artists and national touring exhibitions.

You can also venture to the newly revitalized **Gallery Row** on Postoffice St., three blocks from The Strand, for a "row" of ten more galleries and shops. The **"E" Street Gallery,** 2219 Postoffice St. (409/762-4122), features modern paintings, glass and metal sculptures created by local artists. **The Rainbow Warrior Gallery,** 2217 Postoffice St. (409/763-8683), is another showplace for original work, interpretative pieces, abstract paintings and photography by contemporary Texas and Southwest artists.

For more treasures of Gallery Row, seek out the **Leslie Gallery,** 2208 Postoffice St., which houses local and international original works of sculptural and paper-borne art. **Anderson Gallery,** 2202 Postoffice St., features watercolors by Sally Anderson, oils and watercolors by Richard Kelver, and pastels by Pam Hatch, all of which focus on Galveston.

**Eiband's Gallery,** 2201 Postoffice St. (409/763-5495), in the restored Eiband's Department Store, offers abstract, realistic, and impressionistic oils, watercolor and ceramics, as well as antiques and gift items. Eiband's displays art by the Galveston Art League and local artists. Between Postoffice and The Strand, you'll find the **Barbin Gallery,** 2301 Market (23rd St.) (409/762-1477), which specializes in contemporary iron sculpture and realistic seascapes by artist Oscar E. Barbin as well as a collection of antiques.

*(For complete Galveston art gallery listing, see Arts section.)*

## Strand Restaurants and Pubs

For the best in seaside cuisine, the Strand offers a plethora of restaurants such as the **Mediterranean Chef Restaurant,** 2402 Strand, features Greek food; the **Pasta & Clam Bar,** 2328 Strand, offers a blended menu of Italian and seafood; **Yaga's Tropical Cafe,** 2314 Strand, serves food with a southwestern flair; and **Charley's 517** at the **Wentletrap,** 2301 Strand, offers truly fine dining. Baked flounder parmesan with crab meat, roasted shrimp and herb sauce is delicious to the most particular palate as well as the cabernet braised lamb shanks. The Wentletrap features live jazz music on Friday nights along with hors d'oeuvres. On Tuesdays, the specialty is slow-roasted, herb-crusted prime rib or a specially priced lobster tail and beef tenderloin. If you're thirsting for a beer, go to the **Strand Brewery,** 101 Tremont, just behind Saengerfest Park. There you'll not only benefit from the microbrewery, but also the wood-fired pizza, and the pasta and burgers are good too. The brew pub's upper deck, which offers one of the best views of Galveston Bay, is a perfect place to sample beers brewed on the premises by brewmaster Tyson McCloud. Live music adds to the revelry every weekend. This is also a great place to enjoy the Super Bowl.

If it's morning and you're in the mood for a strawberry waffle, walk over to the **Phoenix Bakery and Coffee House** (a favorite among locals), 214 Tremont, which also serves an array of pastries, sandwiches, and desserts for lunch. Not open for dinner. All baked goods are made fresh on the island. The bakery's shaded courtyard, protected from the weather on three sides by historic buildings, is one of Galveston's favorite morning hideaways. You can also find Mardi Gras' traditional King Cake. The bridal cakes here are something to see and taste! You'll also find the **Rock'N Java Coffee House**, 213 Tremont, across the street for great cappuccino.

For a feel of old New Orleans, try **Bourbon Street**, 215 22nd St. If pizza is what you're hungry for, try **Double Dave's Pizzaworks**, 2002 Postoffice St. (409/762-8400), which offers famous pizza pies as well as strombolis and pepperoni rolls plus 70 beers from 25 nations. At 2120 Strand in the next block, **Todd's Bar and Grill**, offers seafood as the house specialty. For burgers, try **Fullen's Waterwall Restaurant** at 2110 Strand (409/765-6787). **Captain Barnacle Bill's Seafood**, 2102 Strand (409/762-3408), is also a sure place to get fresh Gulf shrimp, crab, fish, and oysters. On Moody (21st St.) you'll find **Dreamers Debbie Pizzaria**, 101 Moody (409/765-9888). Across the street from the Strand Visitor's Center, try **Deli on the Strand**, 2021 Strand (409/762-4629), for sandwiches and ice cream. Also, a good place to go for dessert is **Sa'saparilla**, an authentic Victorian soda fountain where ice cream, yogurt, pizza, soups, and sandwiches are on the menu. For a true candy store and factory, as well as an old-fashioned soda fountain, you must visit **La King's Confectionery**, 2323 Strand (409/762-6100). Everything but the floor is from East Texas drugstores.

**Fitzpatrick's**, 2315 Mechanic (409/765-5914), offers pub-style dining and **The Merchant Prince**, located in the lobby of the Tremont House, provides an elegant setting for a fine dining experience. Fitzpatrick's is an Irish Pub that provides live music on Friday and Saturday nights—the only two nights the Pub is open to the public. For a view of the Port of Galveston and great seafood, stroll to Harborside Dr. (one block off the Strand) and try **Fisherman's Wharf Seafood Grill, Pier 22** (409/765-5708), **Willie G's Seafood and Restaurant, Pier 21**, (409/762-3030) and **Landry's Oyster Bar**, and **Hill's Pier 19 Restaurant and Fish Market**, 20th and Harborside. **The Parlor Bar**, 2314 Strand (409/762-1100), a sophisticated lounge-type setting, is a place to enjoy the company of those you are with while at The Strand. For a Bourbon Street atmosphere, complete with jazz and drinks, try **Nina's Bourbon Street West**, 215 22nd St. (409/762-8894) between Strand and Mechanic Streets, open daily from 4 p.m. to 2 a.m. For a down-home evening, spend time at the **Old Quarter Acoustic Cafe** on Postoffice St. and hear acoustic, country or alternative bands. Music is the main fare here at 413 20th St. (409/762-9199). Open Tuesday–Saturday, 6 p.m.–2 a.m. Nearby is the **Sonrise Gourmet Grind**, an alcohol-free coffee shop, located at 101 22nd St. (409/765-1770).

*(For additional information on nightclubs and pubs, see Nightlife section. For data on Dickens on the Strand or Mardi Gras, see Festivals.)*

# FESTIVALS

## JANUARY

Krewe of Gambrinus King's Day Celebration

## FEBRUARY

Mardi Gras

## MARCH

Home and Garden Show
SpringFest

## APRIL

Annual Upper Texas Coast Birding Festival and Classic
Spirit of Flight Air Show & Walkabout
Galveston Unlimited Air Races and Air Show
Grand Kids Festival

# MAY

Historic Homes Tour Oleander Festival
Cinco de Mayo Beach Festival
Memorial Day Celebration
Annual Art Festival

# JUNE

Juneteenth
AIA Sandcastle Competition
Island Art Festival
Caribbean Carnival Festival

# JULY

Fourth of July Parade and Fireworks

# AUGUST

# SEPTEMBER

Fiestas Patrias

# OCTOBER

Harborfest Galveston

# NOVEMBER

# DECEMBER

Dickens on the Strand

# Mardi Gras

## Galveston Island Convention and Visitors Bureau

2102 Seawall Blvd. • Galveston, TX 77550 • 888/GAL-ISLE
or 409/763-4311 • Fax 409/765-8611 • www.galvestontourism.com
Festival gate admission $10 • Advance tickets $8, available at
Houston-Galveston area Randalls • Children 12 and under free with
paying adult • Momus Parade Bleacher tickets available at area
Ticketmaster locations

## Strand Visitors Center

2016 Strand • Galveston, TX 77550 • 409/765-7834 • 281/280-3907
(Houston)

For two weeks in February, Galveston Island throws a carnival that parallels those of New Orleans and Rio de Janeiro. In an annual event that attracts 600,000 revelers during the 12-day Mardi Gras festival, Galveston makes merriment to feverish pitch with parades, masked balls, art exhibits, music, theater performances, and sporting events.

Although most only remember those recent ones of the past decade orchestrated by Galveston-born preservationist and developer George Mitchell, Mardi Gras has a long history on the Island. Its first recorded event was in 1871 and included a masked ball at Turner Hall (Sealy at 21St.) and a theatrical performance of Shakespeare's *King Henry IV* played by a justice of the peace weighing in at 350 lbs. That first year, the carnival was celebrated on a grand scale, headed by two rival Mardi Gras societies, or "krewes." In fierce competition, both the Knights of Momus, known only by the initials "K.O.M.," and the Knights of Myth sent out elaborate invitations; created spectacular night parades with decorated horse-drawn wagons, all lit by torches; reigned over masked balls; and wore exquisite masked costumes. The procession through downtown Galveston culminated at Turner Hall with a *tableaux* presentation and a grand gala.

Every year a different theme was emphasized with such early motifs as "Dante's Inferno," "The Eras of Chivalry," "Ancient France," "The Crusades," and "Peter the Great." As years passed, parades and balls grew more and more elaborate, and the crowds grew. By 1876, the whole city, "in glittering armor, with music and banners and all the pomp and pageantry that becomes a king," turned out to welcome the Monarch of Revelry—the mighty Momus—who arrived by boat at the Port of Galveston.

By the 1880s, because the street parades became extravagant and expensive, they were suspended for a while until 1890 when the krewe, "Kotton Karnival Kids," brought them back. By 1928, the Kotton Karnival Kids had evolved Mystic Merry Makers and continued their sponsorship of Mardi Gras parades and balls although expense began to become an issue. Years passed, and when the United States found itself plunged into WWII, it became more and more difficult to find the manpower and the materials to continue the lavish carnival. Sadly, the last Mardi Gras to take place was in 1941 until, that is, 40 years later when George Mitchell decided to bring back the celebration to coincide with the opening of his Tremont

House. During that quiet four-decade span, the spark of Mardi Gras stayed kindled through private parties by such hosts as the Maceo family, the Galveston Artillery Club, the Treasure Ball Association, and the Holy Rosary Catholic Church.

Today, 13 participating krewes, the Galveston Park Board of Trustees, corporate sponsors, and private foundations join Mitchell in his continued success in using Mardi Gras to focus on Galveston Island's rich heritage and, at the same time, promote a mid-winter boost of Galveston's economy. The fortnight of rivalry is packed full with eight colorful parades and processions; 20 masked balls and parties; sporting events, including golf and rugby tournaments; a film festival; cooking demonstrations; special art exhibitions; visual, musical, and theatrical performances; mask-making workshops; costume contests; and fashion shows. Every year highlights a different theme. In 1997, for example, the festival was a salute to "Mexico Magnifico!" complete with The Folkloric Ballet of Columbia, the world's largest piñata created by school children from throughout the Houston and Galveston areas, the Masks of Mexico Exhibit, Mexican Contemporary Painting Exhibits, the Mexican Traditional Apparel Exhibit, and the Mexican Film Festival. The 1998 Mardi Gras was based on "The Big Speakeasy."

## Things You Should Know About Mardi Gras Tradition

"Mardi Gras" is French for "Fat Tuesday." The term arose from the custom of parading a fat ox through the streets on Shrove Tuesday, the day before Ash Wednesday, the beginning of Lent. Revelers eat, drink, carouse, and make merry during Mardi Gras in an attempt to satiate the desires of the flesh prior to the abstinence observed during the Lenten season. Although Mardi Gras is a Christian tradition, its origins lie in the ancient Roman custom of merrymaking before a period of fasting.

The date of Mardi Gras depends on the date of Easter. The celebration takes place at the end of a long carnival season beginning Jan. 6, or "Twelfth Night," and is celebrated in many Roman Catholic communities around the world—most notably in New Orleans and Rio de Janeiro.

The order of the day and night is to catch one of the eight Mardi Gras parades, dance in the streets, catch a handful of colorful beads and doubloons, and marvel at the spectacular floats and elaborately costumed revelers. If you want to get into the true spirit of the occasion, wear a mask or carry the hand-held, on-a-stick variety. The more glitter, baubles and beads, the better prepared one is to be swept up in the gaiety of if all. And if you plan to attend the choicest of glittery shindigs, that is, The Tremont House Masked Mardi Gras Ball, you'll see designer capes and gowns, painted faces and shoulders, and elaborate feathered headdresses.

To minimize the hassle of parking, shuttle buses operate at peak times every 15 minutes. A round-trip ticket is usually $2 per person, with children age 4 and younger free. Weekend service includes three shuttles. One runs from 61st St. and Broadway to the Railroad Museum. The second shuttle runs from the West End hotels to the Railroad Museum, 26th and Santa Fe streets. The third runs from the Bolivar Ferry Landing at the end of Ferry Rd. and East End hotels, including the Islander East hotels, the Galvestonian, and La Quinta Inn, to 19th St. and the Strand.

## What is a Krewe?

Each krewe is a nonprofit committee or social club that is dedicated to keeping the spirit of "Fat Tuesday" alive. Each has its own persona and usually is named after a mythological character although many names are chosen based on the personality or make-up of the group. For example, the Krewe of Venus is composed of a Galveston women's group. Together the 13 krewes sponsor the 20 masked balls and the eight torch-lit parades that light up island skies.

## "King Cake"

The "King Cake" or *gallete des rois*, as it is called in French, is a sugar-coated coffee cake ring glazed with the Mardi Gras colors of green, purple, and gold. Gold stands for power or purity of purpose. Purple stands for royalty or justice. Green represents love, friendship, or faith. Each cake contains a hidden "prize," which can be either a dried bean, an almond, or a tiny plastic baby doll. The person who finds the hidden treasure in his piece of king cake is named the "King" or "Queen" and is therefore expected to give the next party. In some circles of friends, the discovery of the "baby" assures good fortune in the new year.

The origin of the "King Cake" is traced back to the celebration of the Twelfth Night, or 12 days after Christmas. The baby hidden in the cake represents the Infant Jesus. The feast is also known as the Three Kings Day, The Feast of the Magi, or Epiphany, and has been considered around the world and through the ages to honor the Three Wise Men who bestowed their gifts on the Christ Child. January 6th is still regarded as the official closing of the Christmas season, the day the tree is taken down.

In Galveston, the selection of King and Queen Gambrinus (Mardi Gras' royalty) is determined by the King's Cake cutting traditional. Also a very popular tradition in New Orleans, King Cakes are big business for bakeries during carnival season. While most are of the coffee-cake variety, some chefs fill the puffed pastry with fancy concoctions of cream cheese or fruit.

The cakes are only available in the Oleander City during Mardi Gras season, which begins with Epiphany and stretches through Mardi Gras Day or "Fat Tuesday." As for the King Cake in other countries, the Germans call it *Driekonigsbrot*, the Danes *Driekonigebrod*, the Dutchmen call it *Driekoningenenbrood*, the Mexicans *Rosca de Reyes*, and the Portuguese call it *Bolo Rei*.

# Parades, Balls, and Special Events

*A listing of parades, balls, and special events follow although some plans change from year to year:*

**Krewe of Gambrinus King's Day Celebration.** Mardi Gras Museum (22nd and Strand) (409/763-1133) 6–9 p.m. Free, open to the public. Traditional King's cake-cutting for selection of King and Queen Gambrinus.

**Z Ball—Coronation of King and Queen Zany III.** South Shore Harbour Resort, Crystal Ball Room (713/996-8656). $75 for members, $85 for guests, $90 at door, $800 corporate tables, drink tickets available. Bands, food, and dessert buffets. Introductions of "Big Mamma."

**Annual Little Miss Teen, Miss Mardi Gras, Ms. and Mrs. Mardi Gras National Pageant.** (409/933-0001), ages 6 months and up. Location changes from year-to-year. Preliminaries and finals one day apart.

**Holy Rosary Catholic Church Annual Mardi Gras Ball and Pageant.** El Mina Shrine Temple, 5500 Seawall Blvd.(409/772-3681 or 409/765-8377). $15 person, BYOB. Live music. Given by the Krewe de Esprit Rosaire.

**Annual Krewe Babalu Ball.** The Grand 1894 Opera House, 2020 Postoffice (409/740-4281) 8 p.m.–1 a.m. $12/person advance, $15 at door. Live music, food, cash bar.

**Mystic Krewe of Aquarius Coronation Ball and Royal Pageant.** Location changes yearly (409/765-8088). 9 p.m.–1 a.m. tickets $35 advance, $40 at door, "Gran Baile" after 5 attire, cash bar.

**Annual King Gambrinus Coronation Ball.** Tremont House, Davidson Ballroom, 2300 Ship's Mechanic Row (409/737-1986) 9 p.m.–1 a.m. $175/member couple, $225/guest couple. Presentation of Krewe of Brew King and Queen and Royal Court, food, black tie/costume.

**Holy Rosary Catholic Church Youth Mardi Gras Ball.** El Mina Shrine Temple, 5500 Seawall, 409/762-2478, 409/772-3681, 409/765-8377 after 5:30 p.m. 7 p.m.–midnight, $5/person. Live music.

**Strand Entertainment District.** Gated area with musical artists (409/765-7834). 8 a.m.-7 p.m. Tickets $8/advance, $10/gate. Food and beverages available, along with T-shirts, beads, and more.

**Texas A&M University at Galveston's Mardi Gras Run.** 20th and Harborside (409/766-1232, 888/RUN-GALV). Kids K, 8:30 a.m.; 5K Run/Walk , 9 a.m.; race day registration $15/$20, post-race party. Presented by Gallery Furniture.

In 1997, the Annual Mardi Gras 5K hosted 5,600 runners and walkers. Sponsored by Texas A&M at Galveston and the Galveston Parks and Recreation, the Port of Galveston and Sisters of Charity, the event begins at the Port of Galveston, east of Pier 21 and runs east past UTMB into the downtown area, proceeding past the Opera House, and finishing at Pier 20 where the festivities begin.

**Mystic Krewe of Aquarius Annual Parade.** Seawall Blvd. at 14th to 59th streets (409/763-0820), noon. Costumed Krewe members led by 14 float captains and the annual royal court, 50 units including 12 spectacular floats, flashy drill teams, 20 high-stepping marching bands, beads, and specially-minted doubloons.

**Annual Galveston Mardi Gras Rugby Tournament.** UTMB Field, 6th and New Strand, (409/740-1151, 409/772-2738) 8 a.m.–5 p.m., free. Teams from Texas and surrounding states participate in preliminary matches, food and beverages available.

**Z Procession.** Historic Strand District, 1 p.m., $10 at door. King Zany III salutes his Queen with the Z Krewe Wild Bunch. Party follows at Estrada's on The Strand.

**Z Procession Parade.** The island's zaniest Krewe stroll through The Strand Historic District, beginning at Ship's Mechanic Row and ending at the Railroad Museum, 25th and Strand. The Z Krewe dignitaries, King Zany I, Big Daddy and the Zoots stop to salute Queen Zany, Big Mamma, and the Zaftigs. Parade usually starts at 1 p.m.

**Mardi Gras Ball for Special People.** Moody Gardens Center (409/744-4673, ext. 318). 1–5 p.m. Free. Sponsored by Hope Therapy. Music, dancing, entertainment, costume contest, refreshments, open to anyone with physical/emotional disability, costume optional, ID badge required.

**Annual Treasure Ball and Royal Pageant Spectator Night.** Sponsored by the Treasure Ball Association, $5 adults, $3 children under 12 years, benefiting O'Connell Catholic School, 7:30 p.m., The Grand 1894 Opera House, 2020 Postoffice St. Tickets available at O'Connell High School, 409/744-5171 after 5:30 p.m.

**Annual Mardi Gras Golf Tournament.** Galveston Island Municipal Golf Course, 99th and Seawall Blvd. (409/744-2366), 1:30 p.m. shotgun start, open to public, $60/person (includes green fee and ½ cart), four-person scramble, prizes to first three teams.

**The San Luis Salute.** The San Luis Hotel (409/744-1500 or 800/445-0090). A sit-down dinner with orchestra serenading in background. Diners also enjoy a fashion show.

**Annual Silk Stocking Ball.** Moody Gardens Conventions Center, One Hope Blvd., (409/765-9891, 409/986-1869, 409/737-3122 after 5 p.m.) 8 p.m.–1 a.m., $45/advance, $600/reserved tables of 10, $75/door. Benefits AIDS related charities of Galveston County, dancing, costume contest, hors d'oeuvres, cash bar, costume or mask.

**Archonettes Auxiliary of Zeta Phi Beta Sorority 3rd Annual Teenage Mardi Gras Ball.** Galveston County Seniors Citizens Center, 2201 Ave. L, (409/740-1158), 7:30-11:30 p.m. $8/person, open to public, ages 13–19, formal, hors d'oeuvres.

**Beta Phi Omega Chapter of Alpha Kappa Alpha Sorority Annual Mardi Gras Ball.** 550 Seawall, El Mina Shrine Temple, (409/762-4084, 409/744-1491). 9 p.m.–1 a.m., tickets $20. Costume or semi-formal with mask, live music, BYOB, setups.

**Bolivar Peninsula Krewe of Lighthouse Parade.** (409/684-5940) Carnivals Around the World.

**Krewe de Esprit Rosaire of Holy Rosary Catholic Church Procession.** 27th and Seawall, 31st and Ave. N., 11 a.m. Family fun procession celebrating 20 years of Mardi Gras for Holy Rosary Catholic Church, Royal Courts, costumed groups, drill teams, marching bands.

**The San Luis Mardi Gras Costume Contest.** The San Luis Hotel, 53rd and Seawall (409/744-1500), 1 p.m. More than 100 costumed participants compete for prizes; celebrity judges, live entertainment and more beginning at noon, parade of entrants along Seawall Blvd.

**Momus Grand Night Parade.** The Strand, Ship's Mechanic Row (800/351-4237, 409/763-4311), 6 p.m. Dazzling illuminated display of floats depicting the theme of the event. The Philadelphia Mummers, college and high school bands, showers of beads, trinkets, specially-minted doubloons, and free trip giveaways.

**The Tremont House Masked Ball.** 2300 Ship's Mechanic Row (409/763-0300, 800/874-2300). Tickets $275/person, $550/couple. Orchestra plays at black-tie masquerade gala, premier viewing of Momus Grand Night Parade, cocktails, and buffet.

**Zestival.** Fitzpatrick's Pub, 2315 Ship's Mechanic Row (409/763-6533), noon, $65/person, Momus Parade viewing, buffet, live band, drink coupons.

**Krewe of Munchkins Parade (Kids Parade).** 1500 block of 25th ending at Railroad Museum (409/762-4401, 744-6668 after 5 p.m.), 2 p.m., $10 entry fee, ages 4–14, 12 floats, beads, doubloons, bands.

**The Galveston Artists Guild.** Randall Room, Rosenberg Library, 2310 Sealy (409/762-4791). Island poets read. Open mike follows scheduled readers.

**U.S. Marine Corps Band Concert.** The Grand 1894 Opera House, 2020 Postoffice (409/765-1894, 800/821-1894), free.

**Annual Pinstripe Pasquinade.** Procession winds through Historic Strand District/Mechanic area. Begins at the Railroad Museum with the Ball High School band to kick it off. Satirical lampoon of corporate teams and business professionals poking fun at themselves; team participants range from vice-presidents to mail clerks. "Pasquinade" means "a satirical lampoon taking place in public." The procession usually begins at 2 p.m. on the first Saturday.

**Krewe of Gambrinus Parade.** Seawall from 12th-59th streets (409/744-6311). King Gambrinus Lights Up The Night with spectacular floats, marching bands, and celebrities.

**Postoffice Street Promenade.** Postoffice from 20th-23rd, free, 6 p.m-midnight. Provided with this parade is an evening of family fun featuring live music, street entertainment, and the All Krewe Processional.

**Knights of Momus Coronation Ball.** The Grand 1894 Opera House, 2020 Postoffice, invitation only. Galveston's oldest Mardi Gras Krewe presents King Frivolous LXXXII and his court of duchesses, dancing to live music, black tie/mask.

**Annual Galveston Rugby Masked Ball.** Galveston Brewery, 25th and Mechanic (409/740-1151, 409/772-2738), $15/person at door. Sponsored by UTMB Galveston Rugby Club, live music, mask/costume.

**Krewe of Gambrinus "Brew HA-HA" After-Parade Party.** Best Western, 59th and Seawall (409/737-1986, 409/744-5900), $10/members, $20/guests. Music, food, and fun.

**Krewe of Thalasar Annual Mardi Gras Ball.** 1912 Winnie (409/763-4645, 713/723-2627, 409/737-2865), 8 p.m.–1 a.m., $25/advanced, $40/door. Galveston's nautical Krewe comprised of former A&M students, doubloon, beads, cups, throws, dancing, hors d'oeuvres and cash bar, creative after-5 attire.

## On Fat Tuesday . . .

**Mystic Krewe of Aquarius Annual Fat Tuesday Procession.** "We End What We Begin." Strand District (409/744-5782), 6:30 p.m. Celebrates the final hours of Mardi Gras.

**Annual Mardi Gras Scholarship Ball and Queen Coronation.** El Mina Shrine Temple, 5500 Seawall (409/762-4873, 409/763-8689), $12. Sponsored by LULAC Council 639, live Tejano music, BYOB, costume/after-5 attire.

# DICKENS ON THE STRAND

## Galveston Historical Foundation

2016 Strand (Strand Visitors Center) • 409/765-7834, 281/280-3907 Fax 409/765-7851 e-mailghf@phoenix.net • $8 adults, $6 kids, under 12 free • Advance tickets $6 per person, available at Randalls Food and Pharmacy in Houston/Galveston area, Market Basket Food Stores in southeast Texas and southwest Louisiana • Everyone in Victorian costume admitted free • First weekend in December, concludes 6 p.m. Sunday

Walk through the ticket gate to "Dickens on the Strand" and find yourself suddenly transported back into the era of Queen Victoria. You'll be surrounded by many of Dickens' immortal characters such as Bob Cratchit and Tiny Tim. You may even get a glimpse of Jacob Marley haunting Ebenezer Scrooge. Your senses will be consumed with the sounds of Christmas handbell choirs, old-time carolers dressed in clothes of the 19th century, and bagpipe bands as they parade down The Strand.

Continuous entertainment on six stages and every street corner between 20th and 25th streets varies from magicians to sword-swallowers to hypnotists and singers. The kids will go wild with excitement when they see "Snow on Sunday," the festival's popular attraction featuring a snow yard for children 10 and under. English bobbies maintain order and direct visitors to Piccadilly Circus and Covent Garden, uniformed Beefeaters make way for Queen Victoria's carriage, and cries of vendors mix with holiday carols. Bonneted ladies in velvet hold hoop skirts as they make their way through the crowd. Victorian gentlemen, distinguished in cutaway coats that match their woolen pants follow with top hats in hand.

For 25 years, the Galveston Historical Foundation has recreated the setting of Charles Dickens' *A Christmas Carol* and the British Empire in The Strand National Historic Landmark District during the first weekend of December. The event, usually graced by the presence of David Charles Dickens, great-grandson of the author, is a lesson in imagery and true Victorian fun for the entire family.

*Events, times and locations are subject to change from year to year.*

Moody Gardens hosts **The IMAX Nutcracker** in 3D. Opens Thanksgiving day and runs through mid-January. This is a favorite of children and adults alike. Set in contemporary London, the take is a non-balletic retelling of E.T.A. Hoffman's classic, *The Nutcracker and The Rat King*, set to the magical score of Tchaikovsky.

**Dickens Feast** in the ballroom of the 1859 Ashton Villa, 2328 Broadway. Cost for a dinner ticket is $50 per person. Reservations required. David Charles Dickens, the author's great-grandson, is usually in attendance.

The excitement of the **East Indies Dock on the London Wharf** at the Texas Seaport Museum is recreated. Explore the 1877 Tall Ship *Elissa* and imagine sailing to exotic ports-of-call. Tickets $2, 10 a.m.–10 p.m. Performances from Gilbert and Sullivan's *H.M.S. Pinafore* can be found on the decks of the historic sailing ship berthed here (separate admission of $5 is required). Admission to the West India Dock includes self-guided tours of the Texas Seaport Museum and the *Elissa*. The Violet Crow Players usually give presentations also of a salty nature onboard the Tall Ship *Elissa* at the cost of about $5. (409/765-7834.)

**The West India Dock at the Texas Seaport Museum** on Pier 21 features dancing, demonstrations of maritime crafts, and tall tales by old salts. Dance a jig to the jaunty tune of a concertina as old salts share tall tales of the West India Dock at the museum. 10 a.m.–5 p.m., Saturday and Sunday.

**"Christmas by Candlelight"** tours at 5, 6, 7, and 8 p.m. at the 1838 Michel B. Menard Home, 1605 33rd St. and the Samuel May Williams Home, 3601 Avenue P. $5 per person (reservations recommended). Flickering candles and kerosene lamps give Galveston's oldest homes a special glow. Costumed hosts welcome guests and guide visitors through antique-filled rooms decorated for the holidays. First weekend in December.

**Evening Handbell Concerts,** 5:30 p.m. at hour intervals at the 1859 St. Joseph's Church, 2202 Avenue K. Cost is $3 per person (reservations recommended). Glow of candles and burnished brass fill painted sanctuary of historic 1859 St. Joseph's Church. Friday and Saturday evenings.

**Morning Tea,** Saturday and Sunday at Ashton Villa with seating every half hour from 8:30 to 11:30 a.m., $14 per person. Freshly-baked scones with marmalade, stone cream, and strawberry jam; flaky sausage rolls; grilled tomatoes; egg and cheese tarts; fresh fruit; assorted teas and coffee.

At the **Strand Theater,** children's theater groups usually perform all day at 2317 Mechanic. Free.

**Royal Menagerie,** an exotic-animal petting zoo at 24th and Strand. Free to all Dickens on the Strand ticket holders.

**Queen's Parade,** Saturday, one of the weekend's premier events starting at noon and proceeding down the Strand again at 2 p.m.

**Dickens Costume Contest** for the best-dressed Victorian lady and gentleman, 4 p.m. Saturday, 21st and Strand. Another contest is held at noon Sunday.

**Snow on Sunday,** a child-pleaser, is for kids 10 and under who are invited to build snowmen and frolic in six inches of snow free of charge. 200 block of 23rd St.

**Run Like the Dickens.** 13th St. and Harborside Dr., Saturday. Annual fun run benefiting the Galveston Ronald McDonald House (409/762-0605).

Call the **Strand Theater** (409/763-4591), the *Grand 1894 Opera House* (409/765-1894 or 800/821-1894) or **Galveston College Theater and Lone Star Performing Arts Association** (800/54-SHOWS, 409/737-3440) for Christmas performances that change yearly.

# HISTORIC HOMES AND BUILDINGS

In the city by the sea, tall pristine steeples reach into the blue horizon along with Gothic gables that seem to say, "Growth can only go up." Ornate grillwork gracefully defines semi-tropical gardens on one side of the island while on the other, a long meandering stretch of Texas beach acts as nature's boundary between man and the sea. Everywhere there is evidence of a time long gone, yet somehow the roots of the Galvestonian's tenacious spirit have held firm in this salty soil. And through the balustrades, around the sculpted stone facings and crop of chimneys that has sprouted since the Great Storm of 1900, the name of architect Nicholas Clayton is whispered. Stately homes, over 1,500 considered historic, and such grand churches as St. Mary's Cathedral Basilica give testimony to man's creations. Graceful curves and curls find their place here by the sea. Altogether, there are 550 landmarks listed on the National Register of Historic Places.

## Galveston Historical Foundation Annual Galveston Historic Homes Tour

2016 Strand • 409/765-7834, 409/281/3907, e-mail: ghf@phoenix.net
Fax 409/765-7851 • $15 person, $13 advance purchase

The first two weekends in May, visitors become guests of the Galveston Historical Foundation's annual historic homes tour of ten homes showcasing Galveston's 19th and early 20th century architecture. This is a chance to walk the rooms of some of the finest privately-owned, restored houses on the island. Some have survived devastating fires, Galveston's 1900 hurricane, and, in some cases, years of neglect. Take this tour and learn about such gifted men as Nicholas Clayton, who designed so many of the private residences and buildings here, as well as the individuals who found their fortune in Galveston and commissioned him to build these residences. Marvel at the turreted stairways, gingerbread trimmed verandas, and Victorian mahogany interiors filled with French antiques, heirloom cut-glass, and hand-painted china. Tickets are $13 per person if purchased by Friday before the first weekend. All tickets will be on sale for $15 per person at each home on the tour; the Strand Visitors Center, 2016 Strand; or Ashton Villa, 2328 Broadway. Tickets are good for both weekends. A complimentary shuttle service is available connecting each home on the tour as well as the 1859 Ashton Villa; The Strand Visitors Center; and The Original Mexican Cafe, 1401 Market. Parking is available in the lot behind Ashton Villa, and on many streets and lots in The Strand National Historic Landmark District. Major credit cards accepted.

Champagne Evening Tours offer champagne and hors d'oeuvres, enjoyed while the sun sets. To order in advance or to inquire about special Champagne Evening Tours, contact the Galveston Historical Foundation.

## The Silk Stocking Historical District
### Along 24th and 25th between Ave. L and Ave. O

Take a carriage ride through this scenic district where many of the city's wealthy merchants and businessmen from the Victorian Period resided. Many of the residences have gone through major face-lifts. It was named for a time when only the well-to-do ladies could afford silk stockings. Note the home at 24th and Avenue L. It's the Sweeny-Royston House, designed by noted architect Nicholas Clayton. Listed on the National Register of Historic Places, it was built in 1885 as a wedding gift from the resident of Ashton Villa, J.M. Brown, for one of his daughters, Matilda. See Strand Visitors Center, the Galveston Island Convention and Visitors Bureau, and Ashton Villa for brochures on the homes of interest. For more information on the district, visit the Galveston Historical Foundation headquarters, 2016 Strand.

## East End Historical District
### 11th to 19th between Market and Broadway (Ave. J)

Also a residential area for those who were in "high cotton," this district dates back as far as the 1850s, but most homes were built between 1875 and the Great Storm of 1900. The entire district is listed on the National Register of Historic Places and is designated as a National Historic Landmark. Pick up a riding and walking tour map that designates the historically significant homes. An audio-tape tour and maps are available for rent at the Galveston Historical Foundation, 409/765-7834.

## 1859 Ashton Villa
2328 Broadway • 409/762-3933 • Mon.–Sat., 10 a.m.–4 p.m. • Sun., noon–4 p.m. • Adults $4, students (7-18) and seniors (65+) $3.50, 6 and under free • Discounts for families and pre-arranged group tours Ballroom available for rent

Ashton Villa, an 1859 Italianate three-story mansion and Broadway Boulevard's only ante-bellum home, stands as a reflection to the success of its wealthy builder, hardware king James M. Brown. Filled with family heirlooms and original art, the house was a lively haunt for the city's social class of the mid 19th century. The main draw here was the intriguing Miss Bettie, Brown's headstrong daughter, who never found a man she considered interesting enough to marry. As Brown was one of the wealthiest men in Texas, Miss Bettie enjoyed his wealth with little regard for Victorian restrictions on the unmarried female. In fact, her modern, very colorful, and headstrong spirit can be felt in her favorite room in the house, the palatial Gold Room, an outstanding example of Gilded Age opulence. It is said that here she entertained her intimate friends and was even known to have drunk champagne from her evening slipper.

Built before the Civil War by Brown, a banker and a contractor who designed homes as well, and the owner of his own brickyard, the home is one of the most impressive historical homes in the city. Saved by the Galveston Historical Foundation in the late 1960s, it was opened as a museum in 1974. The ornate dining room is something to see as well as the furnishings and the Brown family heirlooms.

Each year, the home hosts residents and visitors on the 4th of July for a traditional family picnic and ice cream "crank-off." In December, costumed guests visit the ballroom for an elegant morning tea and a Victorian feast during the Dickens on the Strand holiday festival in early December.

Also here is an audio-visual program on the Great Storm of 1900. A tour of Ashton Villa is truly a glimpse into life among Galveston's rich.

## Bishop's Palace

1402 Broadway • 409/762-2475 • Summer hours: (Memorial Day to Labor Day) Mon.–Sat., 10 a.m.–5 p.m., and Sunday, noon–5:00 p.m. Last daily tour is at 4:45 p.m. • Winter hours: (Labor Day to Memorial Day) noon–4 p.m. daily • $3 person

Built in 1886 for Galveston attorney Colonel Walter Gresham, the home was known originally as Gresham's Castle, which provided a safe haven for many who made their way there during the Great Storm of 1900. Gresham, also a congressional representative who helped found the Gulf, Colorado, and Santa Fe railways, built the home at an estimated cost of $250,000. Built from native Texas granite, white limestone, and red sandstone, the mansion was designed by renown architect Nicholas Clayton. All stones were cut and shaped on the premises. Gresham, upon Clayton's advice, chose magnificent rare woods, such as rosewood, satinwood, white mahogany as well as American oak and maple to create a hand-carved interior masterpiece. Massive sliding doors match woods that adorn facing rooms. Fireplaces and mantels, created all over the world, were used by Victorian craftsmen who literally built rooms to compliment them. The front ballroom's mantel, in fact, won first prize at the Philadelphia World's Fair in 1876. In the music room, the mantel and fireplace are lined with pure silver. Other imported features include a Venetian crystal chandelier, damask wall coverings from London, and an Italian marble fireplace. Bishop Bryne called it "my palace in the sky" while builders call it an architectural wonder.

Now owned by the Galveston-Houston Catholic Diocese, which purchased it in 1923 for Bishop Christopher Byrne, the home is now known as Bishop's Palace. Bishop Byrne lived there until his death in 1950. Today, the Newman Club has its headquarters downstairs. Income from tours are used to maintain the palace and support the Newman Center of the University of Texas Medical Branch and Galveston Community College. The residence is the only building in Texas included on the elite list of architectural masterpieces. It is also among 14 other residences and civic structures that are included in the Archives of the Library of Congress as being representative of early American architecture. In 1956, the Bishop's Place was designated as one of the 100 outstanding buildings in the United States by the American Institute of Architecture.

The Deacon's Den, a gift shop located at the back of the mansion, offers religious articles, souvenirs, gifts, and books, including information and photos about the palace. Call for details. The patio is available for group picnics.

## Moody Mansion & Museum

2618 Broadway/P.O. Box 1300 • Galveston, TX 77553 • 409/762-7668 • Fax 409/762-7055 • Adults $6, seniors (65+), $5, ages 6–18 $3, under 6 free • Mon.-Sat. 10 a.m.–4:30 p.m., Sun. 1 p.m.–4:30 p.m. Closed Mon. in Jan., Feb., and March • Groups welcome daily by reservation

Standing majestically on Broadway Blvd., this red brick mansion, once the home of cotton king, William L. Moody, Jr., was built on a steel frame and equipped to take advantage of one of the first electrical power plants in Texas. Designed by William H. Tyndall and built for the prominent Isle mercantile clad, the Willis family, construction of the turreted 42-room mansion began in 1893 and was completed in 1895. The Moody family bought it shortly after Great Storm. This limestone and brick residence features rare hand-carved wood, stained glass, and Moody family heirlooms. The ballroom is decorated as it was when Mary Moody, noted Galveston philanthropist, made her social debut on December 12, 1911. Mary Moody wed E.C. Northen here on December 1, 1915.

The Moodys, one of the most respected families in Texas during the 19th century, established one of the great financial empires of the 20th century with interests in insurance, banking, hotels, and ranching. Through the Moody Foundation, they contributed generously to the city they loved, and through Mary Moody Northen, Inc., a private foundation, the family has made many contributions to education, health services, the arts, and to historical and cultural institutions.

Located at Broadway and 26th St., the mansion's interior was decorated by Pottier and Stymus, a well-known firm that worked for the White House during Grant's administration and for prestigious names as William Rockefeller, George Westinghouse, Jr., and Thomas Edison. The home opens to the entrance hall of paneled oak with Doric classical design, beamed ceiling, stop-fluted pilasters flanking the doorways, and an oak parquet floor. The parlor, which sets the tone for the entire house, is decorated in an 18th century French style and is decorated with furniture, gilded in the Rococo Revival style. The masculine library, handsome in a decor of the Empire Revival style popular in the 19th century, has seen a world of high-stakes business and powerful politics.

The living room, originally designed as a billiard room, was employed by the Moodys as a family room. Furnished with reading chairs and rockers, this room was the heart of family activity. A Palladian arch dominates the dome that highlights the fireplace. Maple woodwork was grained to look like birch. As for the dining room, it was once the scene of lavish banquets. Overhead, the false-beamed and coffered ceiling has plaster work decorated of rosettes surrounded by the winged *putti* and dolphins. The second floor is a more personal glimpse at the Moodys, where in these private rooms many personal items such as clothing, jewelry, toys, and games are displayed. During the tour, be sure to note the large stained-glass window above the stair landing, which shows a family of four, dressed in classical style, and arms extending in gestures of hospitality.

After her father died in 1954, Mary Moody Northen inherited control of the family empire and soon became known as one of the most powerful business figures in the country. As a result, she earned the title, "the first lady of finance." Her will specified that her home become a museum after her death.

Amenities include a Tea Room, the Museum Gift Shop, and a Visitors Center with changing exhibits. The Tea Room, situated in the family kitchen, is open for meetings and catered luncheons, teas, and progressive dinners and seats 20-50 people.

From mid-November until the first week of January, there is an annual Holiday Display on the first floor which features festive decorations, miniature trains, decorated trees, gingerbread houses, and poinsettias reminiscent of Dickens' time. During Halloween, more than 100 carved pumpkins line the ledges and porches. Locals, dressed in Halloween characters, relate ghost stories at The Great Pumpkin Party, thrown for costumed youngsters.

## 1847 Powhatan House

### 3427 Avenue O • 409/763-0077 • Adults $4, students and seniors, $1

Considered one of Texas' most beautiful Greek revival homes, the 1847 Powhatan House was built by pioneer merchant and Galveston mayor, John Seabrook Sydnor. Sydnor was the largest pre-Civil War slave dealer on the island. This home was the central section of an early hotel before being moved to its present location on Avenue O. The Powhatan House has served as the Galveston Garden Club headquarters since 1965.

## Garten Verein

### Stanley Kempner Park • Ave. O and Ursuline at 27th St.

An exquisite octagon-shaped pavilion is all that remains of Garten Verein, a German social club, circa 1878. The park that surrounds the pavilion is a beautifully landscaped lawn with a croquet course, tennis courts, clubhouse, bowling alleys, and dancing pavilion.

## 1895 Hutchings Sealy Bank Building
### The Strand and 24th St.

The oldest bank in Texas, the 1895 Hutchings Sealy Bank Building is an impressive gray and pink granite, red Texas sandstone and buff-colored brick building. It was designed in the neo-Renaissance style by Galveston architect Nicholas J. Clayton. The three-story structure appears to be a single structure but actually consists of two adjoining structures. The corner structure housed the bank and the eastern building housed the office of Galveston pioneer John Sealy. Born in Pennsylvania in 1822, Sealy came to Galveston in 1846 where he helped launch the Galveston Gas Company and was active in the railroad business. He died in 1884 and left part of his fortune for the construction of a hospital that would treat all patients, regardless of their ability to pay. The John Sealy Hospital is now a large medical facility affiliated with The University of Texas Medical Branch at Galveston. John joined forces with two other businessmen who created the firm of Ball, Hutchings, and Co.

His son, John Sealy II, also occupied the building. A graduate of Princeton, John II took his father's considerable empire and expanded it. With partners, he acquired the Navarro Refining Company of Corsicana and the Security Oil Company of Beaumont. These firms were joined as Magnolia Petroleum and participated in the major oil discoveries of East Texas. In 1925, Magnolia merged with the Standard Oil Company of New York.

John II and his sister, Mrs. R. Waverly Smith, then established the Sealy-Smith Foundation for the benefit of the hospital that bears their father's name. Ball, Hutchings and Company assumed the assets and liabilities of the Commercial and Agricultural Bank, the only chartered bank in Texas prior to the Civil War. Later, George Sealy, a younger brother, joined forces and turned the business from a cotton and commission house to a commercial bank, and in 1879, the bank changed its name to Hutchings, Sealy and Company. After a 1930 merger, the bank became First Hutchings-Sealy National Bank. With its connection to the Commercial and Agricultural Bank, it establishes claim as the oldest bank in Texas.

The bank has played an important role in Galveston's commercial history. George Ball, John Hutchings, John Sealy, and George Sealy were influential in many industries, including railroads, steamship lines, and the wharves. They also established and supported hospitals, schools, and orphanages. In 1985, George and Cynthia Mitchell began a $4 million restoration of this landmark, for use as shops, offices, and a restaurant. The Hutchings-Sealy Bank Building is indicative of Galveston's prosperity in the decade preceding the Great Storm of 1900.

*(For additional information on historic commercial buildings, see The Strand section.)*

# 1838 Michel B. Menard Home

1605 33rd St. • 409/765-7834 or 409/762-3933 • Fri.–Sun., noon–4 p.m. • Adults $6, children (under 12) $3 • Available for rentals and pre-arranged group tours

Galveston's oldest home, this 1838 residence was built by Michel B. Menard, considered a Galveston founder who was instrumental in the settling of Houston. As for the Island, he helped to establish a government as soon as Texas became a republic. Considered a Greek Revival landmark, his home was the site of the first Mardi Gras celebration. Today, the southern style mansion has been restored and is furnished with an impressive collection of Federal and American Empire antiques.

# 1839 Samuel May Williams Home

3601 Avenue P (Bernardo de Galvez) • 409/765-7834 or 409/765-1839 • Sat.–Sun., noon–4 p.m. • Adults $4, children (under 12) $2 • Available for rentals and pre-arranged group tours

Samuel May Williams, the "Father of the Texas Navy," helped build the port that would make Galveston the "Queen City of the Gulf." Williams was Stephen F. Austin's secretary and assistant and became one of the largest landowners in Mexican *Tejas*. When the Texas War for Independence broke out, he used his own money to buy the first ships for the Texas Navy. A sea captain who loved the ocean, he also recruited volunteers for the Texas Army and purchased war supplies. Also Texas' first banker, Williams was also a successful land speculator and considered the "Forgotten Hero of the Texas Revolution."

Built in 1839 during the days of the Republic of Texas, this home, one of the two oldest buildings on the Island, sits as a reminder of a gentler time when gentlemen used utmost curiosity and ladies knew the true meaning of southern hospitality. Its architecture is a blend of a Creole plantation house and a New England sea captain's home. The romantic widow's walk tops the house and gives a panoramic view of the island. Restored and operated as a museum by the Galveston Historical Foundation, this historic home has survived civil war, hurricanes, fires, and economic depressions. It was framed in Maine and shipped by schooner to Texas where it was reassembled for Samuel and his wife, Sarah.

Self-guided tours through the home, which is furnished with many pieces that belonged to the Williams family, enable guests to linger at each room and listen to recorded conversations as they might have occurred among family members. The tour ends with a short film introducing Williams as the "Father of the Texas Navy" and highlighting life on the frontier and at sea. Galveston Historical Foundation holds an Herb Fair here every June. Included are demonstrations on use of herbs in cooking and decorating, tips on how to start and care for herb gardens. A variety of fresh and dried herbs, potpourri, herb-related pottery, art and books are also for sale. For specifics on Herb Fair, call 409/762-3933.

# CHURCHES

## Galveston Historical Foundation's
## Annual Sacred Places Tour

Call the Galveston Historical Foundation • 409/765-7834,
281/280-3907 • $10, reservations recommended • Tickets sold the day
of the tour at Moody Memorial First United Methodist Church, 2805
53rd St., and from 1:30–4 p.m. at 1859 St. Joseph's Church, 2202
Avenue K. Price includes a booklet on Galveston's religious history.

In late January, the Galveston Historical Foundation conducts its annual
Sacred Places Tour, which takes you to the oldest surviving church in
Galveston, the oldest African-American Catholic parish in Texas, and the
second oldest Serbian Orthodox church in the United States. The first
stop is the Moody Memorial First United Methodist Church 2803 53rd
St., where the church choir presents a concert which musically tells the
story of the church's stained glass windows. To see other historically significant churches, you can continue on your own with a foundation publi-
cation containing a map and histories of other old churches and syna-
gogues. Those of particular significance include First Presbyterian, Sacred
Heart Church, St. Mary's Cathedral, St. Joseph's Church, and Trinity Episcopal Church. Some congregations plan musical performances by choirs
or organists.

# Churches and Synagogues for Worship Services

## Apostolic

**Abundant Life**
5801 Ave. S
409/744-7953

## Assemblies of God

**First Assembly of God**
4628 Ave. Q at 47th St.
409/762-4659

**First Latin Assembly of God**
1801 Postoffice St.
409/765-5108

**Iglesia Monte Calvario**
6320 Heards Lane
409/744-2581

## Baptist

**Avenue L Baptist Church**
2612 Ave. L
409/762-8795

**Central Baptist Church**
5310 Ave. R
409/744-4669

**First Union Baptist Church**
1027 Ave. K
409/763-4326

**Gospel Baptist**
3818 Ball
409/765-6409

**Jerusalem Baptist**
2717 Ball
409/763-1748

**Mount Calvary Baptist**
5202 Ave. K
409/744-3772

**Trinity Baptist**
1223 32nd
409/765-5856

**West Point Baptist**
3003 Ave. M
409/762-5642

**Baptist Independent**
Bible Baptist
7021 Heards Lane
409/744-0449

## Baptist-Missionary

**Live Oak Baptist**
1020 32nd. St.
409/765-9488

## Baptist Southern

**First Baptist**
822 Tremont
409/763-1671

**Island Baptist**
11828 Oster Meyer Rd.
409/737-4512

**University Baptist**
426 Winnie
409/765-5258

**West End Baptist**
7402 Stewart Rd.
409/744-3601

## Bible

**Galveston Bible**
424 19th St.
409/765-5007

## Catholic

**St. Mary's Cathedral Basilica**
2011 Church St.
409/762-9611

**Mission Reina De La Paz Church**
7021 51st St.
409/762-2833

**Sacred Heart Church**
1302 Broadway
409/762-6374

**St. Patrick Catholic Church**
1010 35th St.
409/762-9646

**St. Peter's The Apostle Church**
1804 69th St.
409/744-3561

## Christian-Disciples of Christ

**Central Christian Church**
2702 Ave. O ½
409/762-4884

## Christian Science

**Christian Science Society**
2627 Ave. O
409/762-0362

## Church of Christ

**Church of Christ-Broadway Church**
1628 Broadway
409/762-5566

## Church of Latter-Day Saints

**Church of Jesus Christ of Latter-Day Saints**
Galveston Ward 3114
409/744-7938

## Nazarene

**Church of the Nazarene**
2105 5th/Ave. N
409/948-2247

## Episcopal

**Episcopal Campus Ministry at UTMB**
William Temple Episcopal Center
University Chapel of St. Luke the Physician
427 Market
409/762-8641

**Trinity Episcopal Church (founded 1841)**
2216 Ball
409/765-6317

## Full Gospel

**St. Luke Full Gospel Church**
1408 34th St.
409/763-6524

## Greek Orthodox

**Greek Orthodox Church**
19th St. at Ball
409/762-7591

## Jehovah's Witnesses

**Kingdom Hall of Jehovah's Witnesses**
5827 Ave. T
409/744-3877

## Jewish

**Congregation Beth Jacob**
2401 Ave. K
409/762-4545

**Temple B'Nai Israel**
3006 Ave. O
409/765-5796

## Lutheran

**First Lutheran Church (founded 1850)**
2415 Winnie (Ave. G) at 25th St.
409/762-8477

## Methodist

**Moody Memorial First United Methodist Church**
2803 53rd St. at Ave. U
409/744-4526

**Central United Methodist Church**
3308 Ave. 0 ½
409/762-2138

## Non-Denominational

**Church of the Living God**
3315 7 Mile Rd.
409/744-7195

**King of Kings Christian Outreach Center**
6905 Ave. P
409/744-1797

## Pentecostal

**Christian Heritage Church**
2207 67th St.
409/744-1580

## Presbyterian

**Presbyterian Church (founded 1840)**
1903 Church St.
409/762-8638

## Unitarian

**Unitarian Universalist Fellowship**
502 Church St.
409/765-8330

# Schools and Universities

### Texas A & M University at Galveston

Galveston, TX 77554 • Mitchell Campus (main campus): Take 51st St. causeway north to Pelican Island; campus is to the right; home of Texas Clipper • Fort Crockett Campus: Ave. U and 51st. St.; for marine science labs, offices for professors • Waterfront Campus: 8701 Teichman; home of sailing vessels, equipment • 409/740-4400 (all campuses)

This Texas A&M branch is devoted to marine-oriented programs as well as training officers for the U.S. Merchant Marine. The biggest drawing card for tourists is the training ship *Texas Clipper*, built in WWII as a troop carrier. Later converted to a cruise liner, she now serves as a dormitory and floating classroom in the winter and in the summer for maritime cadets. The ship is usually in port from early September to late April, and visitors are welcome aboard on most weekend afternoons. For information on the ship, call 409/740-4559.

### The University of Texas Medical Branch at Galveston

301 University Blvd. • Galveston, TX 77555 • Visitor Information Center is at 6th and Market • 409/772-1011

UTMB has been in existence since 1881 and now has 2,100 students enrolled in its four schools: School of Medicine, School of Nursing, School of Biomedical Sciences, and School of Allied Health Sciences. The largest and oldest medical school in the state, it is a network of seven hospitals and 85 specialty and subspecialty outpatient clinics. Be sure to visit "Old Red," the Ashbel Smith Building at 916 Strand. It was designed by the noted architect Nicholas Clayton in 1890 and houses the McGovern

Hall of Medicine, which contains 12 statues of outstanding contributors to the field of medicine. The building is listed on the National Register of Historic Places.

## Galveston College

**4015 Ave. Q (Administration) • Galveston, TX 77555 • 409/763-6551**

This community college offers a variety of academic and vocational programs. The college hosts a number of musical concerts and drama productions through its Upper Deck Theater, a 150-seat arena theater located in the Fort Crockett building.

# THE ARTS

## THEATER

Thespian lovers can quench their thirst for the theater through **The Grand 1894 Opera House**, the **Lone Star Performing Arts Association**, the **Mary Moody Northen Amphitheater**, and the **Strand Street Theater**. The opera house runs continuous performances that vary from Broadway shows to musical concerts and classical ballet. **Mary Moody Northen Amphitheater** hosts three outdoor musicals in the summer, and two musicals, as part of their Lone Star at the Grand Program, are presented indoors at the **Grand 1894 Opera House**. The **Strand Street Theater**, 2317 Ship's Mechanic Row in the restored 1871 Opperman Building, is a "variety theater" offering comedies, a children's series, movies, musicals, magic, dance, readings, classes, and concerts year-round. The theater offers an intimate setting with only 205 seats, which includes balcony seating. Throughout the year, special productions through these theater sources coincide with such events as Mardi Gras and Dickens on the Strand, making Galveston Island a cultural center.

### The Grand 1894 Opera House

**Box Office: 2020 Postoffice St. • 409/765-1894**
**www.galveston.com/arts/grand.html**

Continuous performances vary from top Broadway productions to the annual *Nutcracker* and *A Tuna Christmas*, to battles between big bands and singers, to the ballet and the symphony.

### Galveston Island Outdoor Musicals
### Mary Moody Northen Amphitheater

**Galveston Island State Park/14528 Stewart Rd. • 409/737-3440**

Truly wonderful musical alive with spectacular lighting, costuming, and star-studded performances, this is a theater experience that is a must.

However, if you plan to attend a show in this open-air amphitheater, located on the east side of the island, be sure to bring mosquito repellent with you. These marshy pests can ruin your evening.

## Lone Star Performing Arts Association

14528 Stewart Rd. • Galveston, TX 77554 • 409/737-1744

The association sponsors several performances including those presented by the Galveston Island Outdoor Musicals. Call for yearly schedule.

## Strand Theater

2317 Ship's Mechanic Row • 409/763-4591

This variety theater offers a gamut of specialty viewing—celluloid classics, children's musicals, live performances, and current Cannes Film Festival pieces.

## Galveston Ballet

2401 Winnie • 409/763-8620

## Galveston Symphony Orchestra

2127 Strand • 409/762-2787

## Upper Deck Theater

5001 Ave. U • Tickets: 409/744-9661, 900/547-4697

The Galveston College Theater's yearly season is presented at the Strand Theater. These productions are presented in partnership with Lone Star Performing Arts Association, Inc., a resident professional theater. You may purchase tickets direct at The Outdoor Amphitheater, Mon.–Fri. 9 a.m.–5 p.m., 14528 Stewart Rd. or the Strand Street Theater one hour before show time, subject to availability. For the Strand location, there is complimentary parking at Moody National Bank, 24th and Postoffice.

# ART GALLERIES

Located in the newly revitalized **Arts and Entertainment District** along Postoffice Street from 20th to 23rd streets, art galleries thrive. Every six weeks on a Saturday evening these galleries get together to introduce visitors to artists who are old and new, local or world-renown. Dress is casual and walking shoes are recommended as you may decide to visit several galleries at a time and some are a distance. There is a free rubber tire trolley that makes regular rounds of the galleries and is a welcome sight for many of the walkers. All galleries provide snacks and beverages. Hours are 6–9 p.m. Many of the stores, shops, coffee houses, and restaurants are open for your shopping and dining enjoyment. For dates and list of galleries participating in the event, call the Galveston Arts Center or the Galveston Island Convention and Visitors Center (409/763-4311 or 888-GAL-ISLE).

## Galveston Arts Center

2127 Strand • 409/763-2403 • Mon.–Sat., 10 a.m.–5 p.m. • Sun., noon–5 p.m.

The center offers the work of emerging and established regional artists in all types of media.

*In the Strand the revitalized Gallery Row on Postoffice Street is just three short blocks from The Strand and houses the following galleries:*

## E Street Gallery

2219 Postoffice St. • 409/762-4122

This gallery features contemporary paintings, and glass and metal sculptures by local artists.

## Rainbow Warrior Gallery

2217 Postoffice St. • 409/763-8683

Contemporary art, sculptures, hand-crafted jewelry, unique gifts.

## Leslie Gallery

2208 Postoffice St. • 409/763-6370

Original art, fine prints, paper-borne art, and custom framing.

## Anderson Gallery

2202 Postoffice St. • 409/763-2265

Sally Anderson shows her watercolors here as well as oils and watercolors by Richard Kelver and pastels by Pam Hatch. They focus on Galveston scenes.

## Eibands Gallery

2201 Postoffice St. • 409/763-5495

This gallery is located in the restored Eiband's Department Store and offers abstract, realism, and impressionism oils, watercolor and ceramics, as well as antiques and gift items. Eiband's displays art by the Galveston Art League and local artists.

## Two Friends Gallery

2301 Strand • 409/765-7477

Contemporary crafts in glass, clay, fiber, and metal (many local and regional).

## Don Rouse's Wildlife Gallery

2314 Strand • 409/763-1391

Don Rouse features original art, prints, and sculptures by Texas and nationally known artists.

## Barbin Gallery

2301 Market St. • 409/762-1477

The Barbin Gallery specializes in contemporary iron sculpture and realism seascapes by artist Oscar E. Barbin and also includes antiques.

## Artists Loft Gallery

2326 Strand, second floor • 409/765-6035

Group exhibitions in the landmark Hutchings-Sealy Building.

## Encore Gallery

2120 Postoffice St. • 409/762-7780

## Admiralty Marine Model Gallery

1825 Rosenberg • 409/766-1777

Museum-quality ship models, nautical art, sculptures, and gifts.

## J. Bangle Galleries

2319 The Strand • 409/763-6161

If you're in the market for art based on Galveston architecture, the port, or the Tall Ship *Elissa*, see this gallery, which also offers antiques, accents, and custom picture framing.

## Galveston Gallery

1825 Rosenberg (25th and Ave. P) • 409/763-6116

Watercolors, oils and canvas, mixed media, sculpture and fiber art in subjective, abstract, and contemporary styles—all by Texas artists.

# ACCOMMODATIONS

Galveston Island offers a variety of accommodations including luxury hotels, economical motels, condominiums, beach house rentals, and historic bed and breakfasts.

## Key to Symbols

*Rates are subject to change and may not reflect weekends, holidays, festivals, and special events.*

$ (under $55)
$$ ($55-$75)
$$$ ($75-$125)
$$$$ ($125 and up)
W Wheelchair accessible
P Pool on grounds
B Beachfront
L Lounge

## Hotel Galvez

### 2024 Seawall Blvd. • 409/765-7721, 800/392-4285, 800/HERITAGE
### $$$–$$$$

Historic Hotel Galvez, opened in 1911 at the cost of over $1 million, reigns as an elegant first-class hotel that stands guard over Galveston Island. Once known as the "Playground of the Southwest," the waterfront Galvez was once the stomping grounds for scores of political and movie celebrities, including Presidents Franklin Roosevelt, Dwight D. Eisenhower, Lyndon B. Johnson, and John F. Kennedy; General Douglas MacArthur; Phil Harris; Frank Sinatra; Jimmy Stewart; Alice Fay; "Wrong Way" Corrigan; and Howard Hughes. Listed on the National Register of Historic Places, this Grande dame offers old-world luxury throughout its 228 guest rooms, Bernardo's Restaurant, giant meeting rooms, and The Veranda, a romantic spot for light fare and cocktails. The new pool with swim-up bar and Jacuzzi and a Seaside Grill lush with tropical gardens also add to the hotel's charm.

Dubbed in the old days as the "Queen of the Gulf," Hotel Galvez was named for the Spanish colonial governor, Bernardo de Galvez, who first chartered the Texas Gulf Coast and also the city's namesake. Built in the aftermath of the Great Storm of 1900, this Spanish Colonial Revival hotel has become a symbol of the courageous spirit of island survivors who made it through the 1900 storm. In that time of rebirth, the hotel had a barber and candy shop, drug store, soda fountain, and Gentleman's Bar and Grill. Roller chairs lined the entrance for those wanting to take short trips along the now famous Seawall Blvd. In 1918, the hotel registry showed more than 400 guests staying overnight with rates starting at $2 per night. In fact, according to *Hotel Monthly* in 1921, Hotel Galvez was the "best arranged and most richly furnished seaside hotel in America." And along with the throng, came the bathing beauties. In the 1920s, the first bathing beauty contests in the nation were held at the six-story hotel with future movie stars Joan Blondell and Dorothy Lamour as participants. Later, the hotel served in a more official capacity as a living and working facility for the U.S. Coast Guard during WWII. Among the hotel's many owners was Galveston's W.L. Moody, Jr. and the renown heart surgeon Denton Cooley.

Now owned by Galveston's number one couple, George and Cynthia Mitchell and managed by Grand Heritage Hotels, Hotel Galvez has just gone through another major renovation. The hotel's grand seawall entrance greets visitors with towering palms and landscaped grounds lush with greenery. Guest rooms and the three suites, all offering panoramic views of the water, have been redecorated in quality wallpapers and paint in seaside hues of peach, ivory, and seafoam green. The two-level Penthouse Suite, the setting for the marriage of old-time stars Phil Harris and Alice Faye, features a game room complete with a pool table downstairs, and a private bedroom with a king-size canopy bed, living room, and upstairs dining room. Special penthouse amenities include two full baths, a full bar, four telephones, two television sets, and a sitting room that can accommodate up to 70 guests.

Guests of Hotel Galvez have several dining and entertainment options. **Bernardo's** is the hotel's main dining room, seating 145 and featuring traditional and nouvelle cuisine. Located off the lobby, the restaurant is decorated in shades of teals, greens, and pinks. Its airy design provides extensive views of the beach. Bernardo's is open daily for breakfast, lunch, and dinner. If you like to dance or listen to live music, **Club Galvez** features popular local entertainers Friday and Saturday evenings. Guests can enjoy appetizers, sandwiches, and salads in the comfortable antique mahogany-and-brass trim bar. The outdoor **Seaside Grill** also provides cocktails, lunch, and dinner fare during the summer.

All guests receive membership privileges to Galveston Country Club's 18-hole golf course and tennis courts. If you have a dog and wish to bring him along, ask about their dog program. The fixed-rail Galvez Island Trolley chugs to the front door to take guests on a nostalgic tour of historic homes and the Strand Historic District.

# The Tremont House

**2300 Ship's Mechanic Row • 409/763-0300 or 713/480-8201 or 800/874-2300 • $$$$**

Awarded four stars by Mobil Travel Guide, this 117-room luxury hotel, in the heart of Galveston's Strand National Historic Landmark District, rules over the port side of the Island. Also a property of the Mitchells, this posh accommodation is the third hotel to bear the name of "Tremont" in Galveston although the present hotel is not located on the original spot of the first at Postoffice St. and Tremont. Today's hotel, however, is just around the corner on Ship's Mechanic Row in the 1879 Leon & H. Blum Building, a commercial building, which was once a wholesale house and then in 1923, the home of the *Galveston Tribune* for 40 years. Transformed at the cost of about $12 million, the Tremont House offers five restaurants, three bars, and 13 meeting rooms accommodating 10 to 800. Within walking distance is a host of restaurants, retail shops, art galleries, museums, and Pier 21, home of the Tall Ship *Elissa*.

The Mitchells chose the century-old name because they knew the history of the old 1839 Tremont, known in its day as the largest hotel in the Republic of Texas and in the state of Texas for years. A glimpse into the century-old guest register reveals signatures of General Sam Houston, Ulysses S. Grant, Clara Barton, Edwin Booth, and Buffalo Bill. Houston, in fact, delivered his last public address here. Cotton merchants negotiated deals; Sioux Chiefs sampled southern meals; six presidents came to call; Victorian gentry attended grand balls; and soldiers from three wars returned to homecoming banquets. In a great loss to the Island, the first Tremont burned in 1865 in a fire that swept through the entire Strand District but was replaced seven years later by a new elegant Victorian-designed Tremont, majestic with grand double stairway, Corinthian columns, atrium and skylight, not unlike today's new Tremont. Before being closed and demolished in 1928, the second Tremont gained its place in history by providing shelter to refugees of the Great Storm of 1900, a national catastrophe that claimed 6,000 lives.

A member of Historic Hotels of America, The Tremont building is dressed in a Neo-Renaissance facade, reaches four stories high, and takes up a full block. The elegant architectural details, the narrow windows crowned by voussoirs, a cornice topped with an oculus, and a ground-floor arcade with open bays and stately masonry piers, set the mood for the interior's white stucco skylight atrium with palm trees growing from grated openings at its base. Guest rooms on the perimeter of the atrium open through glazed French doors onto ironwork balconies. Interior bridges connect the upper-level hallways. Birdcage elevators carry guests to the upper floors.

Guest rooms on the upper three floors incorporate 19th century charm with 20th century comfort. Decorated in crisp black and white, most rooms have 14-foot ceilings and 11-foot windows. Custom-crafted furnishings include white enamel and brass beds with crisp white bed linens, airy lace curtains, specially-woven black-and-white rugs on polished hardwood floors, massive armoires, and in the adjoining baths, European towel warmers, personalized toiletries and tiles hand-painted in Italy. The Belmont Suites, with soaring 14-foot ceilings and illuminated by 11-foot windows, are the ultimate in comfort and taste with pressed tin ceilings, Jacuzzi bathtubs, four-poster beds, and pull-out desks.

For light fare and drinks, be sure to visit the **Henry Toujouse Bar,** located in the atrium on the grand floor of the Tremont. This beautiful rosewood bar, a historical find, dates back to 1872, when a young Frenchman by the name of Henry Toujouse found work at the Opera House Saloon, located in the basement of the Tremont Opera House. **The Merchant Prince,** an intimate restaurant named for Leon Blum, the premiere Island merchant at the turn of the century, sits in an airy nook facing the palm-lined atrium. Continental cuisine, including soft shell crab, grilled shrimp, blackened swordfish, pasta and medallions of veal, is the gourmet fare. The restaurant is open for all meals and Sunday brunch. Guests may also choose from Charley's 517 at the Wentletrap, in the same block and sister property of The Tremont House, which also serves outstanding continental cuisine. Although there is no pool, one is available to guests at a nearby hotel. The fixed-rail Galveston Island Trolley stops at the front door of The Tremont House, taking visitors on a tour past historic homes and the Seawall. Although owned by George and Cynthia Mitchell, Grand Heritage Hotels manages operations here.

The Mitchells also own the **Harbor House,** a new 42-room accommodation located on Pier 21. This beautiful new inn is located at Pier 21 next to the Great Storm of 1900 Museum, the Mosquito Fleet, and the Ocean Star Energy Museum.

## The San Luis Resort and Conference Center

**5222 Seawall Blvd./53rd and Seawall Blvd. • 409/744-1500, 800/445-0090 • $$$–$$$$**

Located on the 22-acre site of Galveston's historic Fort Crockett, The San Luis Resort and Conference Center is the largest resort hotel and condominium complex in Galveston featuring 500 rooms, all with balconies and magnificent, unobstructed views of the Gulf. This 16-story hotel is filled with designer fabrics and carpets that carry over into each room, which is furnished with overstuffed chairs, a desk, and phones with fax/modem capabilities. An elegant 4,000-sq.-ft. glass-enclosed lobby and promenade make up the grand entry that is filled with ever-present music from a baby grand. Tropical plants and soft seaside colors of pale beiges, pinks, and greens introduce the island motif that is carried throughout the hotel, including the luxurious swimming pool. Six gazebos with Mediterranean-style red-tile roofs are scattered throughout the property offering guests a true resort feel.

Owned by restaurant giant, Galvestonian Tilman J. Fertitta, the hotel complex encompasses 250 guest rooms in the main tower with the next-door sister properties, including the Galveston Island Hilton, adding 150 rooms and 110 condos. The 40,000 square-foot conference center is made up of 12 rooms, equipped with ergonomic chairs, individual climate controls, adjustable lighting, and tackable wall surfaces. The Hilton, formerly the Inn at San Luis, is complete with a newly designed lobby, bar, outdoor pool, and swim-up bar. Also there is the **Palm Court**, a cafe-style restaurant offering breakfast, lunch, and dinner in a casual and relaxed atmosphere.

Sports lovers may golf at a nearby golf course, swim, exercise in the weight room, or play on-site tennis. If you would rather stay indoors, there is a private lounge where there are two billiard tables, a shuffleboard table, and electronic dart boards.

# BED AND BREAKFASTS

For a sampling of historic bed and breakfast accommodations on Galveston Island, two descriptions follow. However, for a complete guide, see *Texas Bed and Breakfast* by authors Gail Drago, Marjie Mugno Acheson, and Lyn Dunsavage. (Gulf Publishing Co.)

## Gilded Thistle

**1805 Broadway • 409/763-0194 or 800/654-9380 • Fax 409/763-3941 • http://www.houston.–TX.NET/lodging/Gilded Thistle/ E-mail: gilded@houston–TX.Net. • $$$$**

The Gilded Thistle, one of the first bed-and-breakfasts on Galveston Island, opened over a decade ago and is still in business, testimony to its success as a guest-pleaser. Built in 1893 and historically known as the Baily-Phillips home, this accommodation was named after the hearty, prickly plant that sheds its ugliness when it blooms along Gulf Coast shores. A survivor of the Great Storm of 1900, this great old house sits on Broadway Blvd. and is an elegant example of Queen Anne architecture with porches, balconies, and transoms, a popular style on the Island over 100 years ago. Resident antiques mix with comfortable elegance to make every guest feel at home.

Guests enjoy amenities that include an evening glass of wine, soft drinks, candy, filtered water, a nighttime snack, a morning coffee tray, as well as a gourmet breakfast. Businessmen have technology privileges, complete with on-line hook-ups. No pets or children. Smoking in designated areas only.

## Madame Dyer's Bed and Breakfast

**1720 Postoffice St. • 409/765-5692 • $$$–$$$$**

In 1889 the noted Galveston architect Nicholas Clayton, creator of many island structures such as Bishop's Palace, Grace Episcopal Church, and the W.L. Moody Building, built a grand residence for Dr. Arthur F. Sampson, a respected physician and surgeon. Characterized by its double, wrap-around galleries and stick-style balustrades, this two-story residence is today known as Madame Dyer's Bed and Breakfast, which is within walking distance of the Strand.

Filled with a combination of period and eclectic furnishings, this B&B features rich wall coverings and fabrics, great natural light, and arty dried flower arrangements. Guest rooms include romantic grand bay windows as a backdrop for antique English furnishings, tiled fireplace, and mirrored oak mantels. Spacious balconies look down onto butterfly-laden gardens.

Guests enjoy morning coffee (gourmet or regular) or tea at the buffet bar on the landing. Breakfast consists of meat, potato and egg dishes; fruit; breakfast spreads; muffins; and traditional morning beverages. The city's horse-drawn carriages pass by regularly, and for a fee, passengers can hop a ride into Galveston's past. Children over 12 are permitted, but no pets. Smoking is allowed outside only.

# BEACHFRONT HOTELS AND CONDOMINIUMS

## Best Western Beachfront Inn

5914 Seawall Blvd. • Galveston, TX 77551 • 409/740-1261, 800/528-1234 • $–$$$$ • 151 rooms • W/P/B

## By the Sea Condominiums

7310 Seawall Blvd. • Galveston, TX 77551 • 409/740-0905, 800/666-0905 • $$$–$$$$ • 104 rooms • P/B

## Casa Del Mar Beachfront Suites

6102 Seawall Blvd. • Galveston, TX 77551 • 409/740-2431, 800/392-1205 • $$–$$$$ • 180 suites • P/B

## Comfort Inn

2300 Seawall Blvd. • Galveston, TX 77550 • 409/762-1166, 800/221-2222 • $–$$$$ • 120 rooms including suites • W/P/B/L

## Days Inn

6107 Broadway • 409/740-2491, 800/325-2525 • $–$$ • W/P

## Econolodge

2825 61st • 409/744-7133, 800/424-4777 • $$ • W/P

## Gaido's Seaside Inn

3828 Seawall Blvd. • Galveston, TX 77550 • 409/762-9625, 800/525-0064, 713/280-3995 • $–$$$$ (depending upon the season)
102 rooms including suites • W/P/B/L

## Galveston Island Hilton Resort

5400 Seawall Blvd. • 409/744-5000, 800/HILTONS • $$$–$$$$
154 rooms • W/P/B/L

## The Galvestonian Condominiums

1401 E. Beach Blvd. • 409/765-6161, 713/280-3929 • $$$–$$$$
58 suites • W/P/B

## Holiday Inn On The Beach

5002 Seawall Blvd. • 409/740-3581, 800/452-6002, 713/222-2032
$$$–$$$$ • 158 rooms • W/P/B/L

## Hotel Galvez

2024 Seawall Blvd. • 409/765-7721, 800/392-4285 • $$$–$$$$
228 rooms • W/P/B/L

## Howard Johnson Suites

2525 Jones Dr. at Scholes Field • 409/740-1155, 800/446-4656
$–$$$ • 67 rooms • W/P/B/L

## Inverness By The Sea

7600 Seawall Blvd. • Galveston, TX 77551 • 409/740-5607,
800/460-6378 • $$$$ • 51 suites • P/B

## Islander East Condominiums

415 East Beach Dr. • Galveston, TX 77550 • 409/765-9301,
888/475-3327 • 40 suites • $$–$$$$ • W/P/B

## La Quinta Galveston

1402 Seawall Blvd. • Galveston, TX 77550 • 800/531-5900,
409/763-1224 • $$–$$$$ • 117 rooms including suites

## Motel 6

7404 Broadway • Galveston, TX 77551 • 409/740-3794,
505/891-6161 • $ • 17 rooms • W/P

## Ramada Inn Resort

600 Harborside Dr. • Galveston, TX 77550 • 409/765-5544
$$–$$$$ • 232 rooms • W/P/L

## The Reef Resort

8502 Seawall Blvd. • Galveston, TX 77554 • 409/740-0492
$$–$$$$ • 36 rooms including suites • P/B

## The Riviera on West Beach

11949 FM 3005 • Galveston, TX 77554 • 409/737-2556,
800/880-2554, 713/280-3969 • $$$$ • 17 rooms including suites
W/P/B

## San Luis Resort Hotel and Conference Center

5220 Seawall Blvd. • 409/744-1500, 800/445-0090 • $$$–$$$$
250 rooms include balconies overlooking the Gulf • W/B/P/L

## Seascape Condominiums/AB Sea Sales and Rentals, Inc.

10811 San Luis Pass Rd. • Galveston, TX 77554 • 409/740-1245
Fax 409/740-2711 • 17 rooms including suites • $$–$$$$ • W/B/P

## Victorian Condo-Hotel and Conference Center

6300 Seawall Blvd. • Galveston, TX 77551 • 409/740-3555,
713/480-0436, 800/231-6363 • www.galveston.com/accom/victorian.html
230 rooms including suites • $$–$$$$ • B/P/L

# HOTELS IN OR NEAR THE STRAND HISTORIC DISTRICT

## Harbor House

#28, Pier 21 • Galveston, TX 77550 • 409/763-3321, 800/874-3721
42 rooms (on harborside) • $$$-$$$$ • W/L

## The Tremont House

2300 Ship's Mechanic Row • 409/763-0300, 800/874-2300,
713/480-8201 • 117 rooms including suites • $$$–$$$$
(depends on special events) W/L/pool privileges at Hotel Galvez

## Ramada Inn Resort

600 Harborside Dr. • 409/765-5544, 800-2RAMADA
$$–$$$$ • W/P

# BED AND BREAKFASTS

**Away At Sea Inn/Jacuzzi Suites (1877)**
1127 Church • 409/762-1668, 800/762-1668 • $$$–$$$$

**Bayview Bed and Breakfast With Boat Pier**
P.O. Box 1326 • Galveston, TX 77553 • 409/741-0705 • $$–$$$$

**Carousel Inn (1886)**
712 10th St. • 409/762-2166 • $$$–$$$$

**Coppersmith Inn (1887)**
1914 Ave. M • 409/763-7004, 800/515-7444 • $$$–$$$$

**Gilded Thistle (1892)**
1805 Broadway • 409/763-0194, 800/654-9380 • $$$$

**The Herb House Bed and Breakfast (1928)**
3815 Ave. P • 409/762-4287 • $$$–$$$$

**The Inn at 1816 Postoffice (1886)**
1816 Postoffice St. • 409/765-9444 • $$$–$$$$

**Inn On The Strand (1856)**
2021 Strand • 409/762-4444 • $$$$

**Madame Dyer's Bed and Breakfast Inn (1915)**
1720 Postoffice St. • 409/765-5692 • $$$–$$$$

**Michael's Bed and Breakfast Inn (1915)**
1715 35th St. • 409/763-3760, 800/776-8302 • $$$–$$$$

**The Queen Anne Bed and Breakfast (1905)**
1915 Sealy • 409/763-7088, 800/472-0930 • $$$–$$$$

**Victorian Bed and Breakfast Inn (1899)**
511 17th St. • 409/762-3235 • $$$–$$$$

# BEACH/BAY HOME RENTALS

*The following companies offer beach/bay home rentals. Price ranges are subject to change. They may not reflect weekends, holidays, festivals, or special events. Call for daily, weekly or monthly rates.*

## All On Beach Rentals

6610 Steward Rd., #117 • Galveston, TX 77551 • 409/766-0009, 800/227-5883 • $170–$695

## Castaways Resort Properties, Inc.

16510 FM 3005 • Galveston, TX 77554 • 409/737-5300, 800/380-5100 • $365–$3,500

## Century 21 Bay Reef Realty

16708-C San Luis Rd. • Galveston, TX 77554 • 409/737-2300, 800/527-7333, 281/280-3909 • $440–$3,000

## Coldwell Banker Lighthouse Realty

8610 Seawall Blvd. • Galveston, TX 77554 • 409/740-4040, 713/280-3990 • $400–$1,500

## Galveston Rentals and Management

201 Seawall Blvd. • Galveston, TX 77550 • 409/765-8600, 888/242-5837 • $400–$2,000

## Gary Greene Realtors

13450 FM 3005 • Galveston, TX 77554 • 409/737-5200, 800/880-9697 • $600–$3,500

## Menotti Properties

12201 San Luis Pass Rd. • Galveston, TX 77554 • 409/737-4700, 713/280-3939, 800/256-7754

## Pirates Beach and Cove Rentals

The Woodlands Corp. • 4179 Pirates Beach • Galveston, TX 77554 409/740-6444, 713/718-9998, 800/789-4401 • $425–$4,000

## Prudential Galveston Realty

16602 San Luis Pass Rd. • Galveston, TX 77554 • 800/666-3561
$548-$3,255

## Re/Max Galveston

12202 San Luis Pass Rd. • Galveston, TX 77554 • 409/737-3777,
713/280-3999 • Fax 409/737-3511 • $250–$1,520

## Sand 'N Sea Properties, Inc.

11348 FM 3005 • P.O. Box 5165 • Galveston, TX 77554
409/737-2556, 713/280-3969, 800/880-2554 • $550–$3,000

## Wolverton & Associates Realty

17614 San Luis Pass Rd. • P.O. Box 5255 • Galveston, TX 77554
409/737-1430, 800/445-1396 • $400–$3,000

# R.V. PARKS

## Bayou Haven R.V. Park

6310 Heards Land • Galveston, TX 77551 • 888/744-2837
$15.50–$18.50 per night • 84 spaces/84 full hookups/tents welcome
restrooms and showers/laundry facilities/picnic area/shelters/
groceries/public telephones

## Dellanera R.V. Park

10910 San Luis Pass Rd.• Galveston, TX 77554 • 409/740-0390,
409/740-0387 • $15–$18 • 84 spaces/51 full hookups/33 partial
hookups • restrooms and showers/laundry/picnic area/shelters
groceries/public telephones/recreation room

## Galveston Island R.V. Resort

2323 Skymaster • Galveston, TX 77551 • 409/744-5464
$13.50–$15 • 60 spaces/60 full hookups • restrooms/laundry/picnic
area/shelters • public telephones/recreation room

## Galveston Island State Park

14901 FM 3005 • Galveston, TX 77554 • 409/737-1222
$12–$15 • 180 spaces/170 partial hookups • 10 screen shelters/
restrooms/showers/picnic area/shelters/public telephones

# RESTAURANTS

Galveston competes with southern Louisiana in offering the best seafood dinners on the planet. Scrumptious seafood platters, steaming bowls of crab and shrimp gumbo, and stuffed flounder coupled with dirty rice leave diners wanting the recipes.

However, the palate here is as varied as an international city and offers a complete range of fare, including Continental, Mexican, Chinese, Japanese, Cajun, Italian, and Texas barbecue. But whatever your taste, whether it's boiled crawfish or a simple burger, the island offers a host of restaurants that suit every taste, and most have a great view of the water or the Strand.

## Key to Symbols

$         Inexpensive/under $7
$$        Moderate/$7–$15
$$$       Expensive/$16–$29
$$$$      Very expensive/$30 and up

*All prices are subject to change. They reflect dinner for one, exclusive of liquor, tax, and tip.*

## SEAFOOD

### Clary's

**8509 Teichman • 409/740-0771 • $–$$$ • Closed Mondays**

One of Galveston's best-kept secrets, locals go here to savor shrimp cocktail, clam chowder, grilled oysters, and fried fish, all prepared to perfection. Clary's is located near the causeway entrance and has been family-owned and operated for more than 18 years. Owner Clary is from southern Louisiana, and his food testifies to the richness of that Acadian lifestyle. Without a doubt he knows the true definition of roux, and his gumbo is testimony to that fact. The menu at Clary's, though, also reflects a continental fare that is nothing short of elegant. Clary's grilled oysters, for example, are just as scrumptious as his special butter lump crab meat, complete with chopped scallions, bacon, grated Cheddar cheese, and melted butter. Seasoned baked crab with flame broiled shrimp is also a specialty.

The setting is tranquil, a bulkhead on an inlet off Offatt's Bayou, with shrimp boats gliding by on their way to and from the Gulf. Blissful, civilized surroundings with dinner music from a classical guitar makes dining here a memorable evening indeed. Coats for men aren't required but suggested.

## Gaido's
### 3800 Seawall (39th and Seawall) • 409/762-9625 • $$–$$$ • Open seven days

Founded in 1911 by Italian immigrant San Jacinto Gaido, this premier restaurant is still operated by family members, including great grandsons Mickey and Paulie Gaido. With seafood as the specialty, Gaido's, a Galveston tradition, offers only the freshest from the sea, which is prepared fried or grilled. The only trouble you'll have here is trying to decide what to order. The stuffed flounder is nationally known as well as the shrimp bisque, found on the appetizer menu. As for salads, the lump crab meat salad is unbelievable as well as the three house-prepared dressings. If you have room for dessert, the pecan pie is a must.

Gaido's has served such prestigious diners as George Bush, Lady Bird Johnson, the rock band ZZ Top, Earl Campbell, Nolan Ryan, the most famous "Tarzan" Johnny Weismuller, Alfred Hitchcock, and Boxer Sugar Ray Leonard. Most know Gaido's by its giant blue crab that sits on the roof. Go early or late, however, as the lines are always long. Daily specials change with the season, but it doesn't matter what is served as each is exceptional. Here's your chance to throw dieting to ocean winds.

## Landry's Seafood House at The San Luis Resort
### 5310 Seawall • 409/744-1010 • $$–$$$

Landry's Seafood House offers outdoor dining on Seawall Blvd. with the ocean in clear view. Its signature seafood toppings such as Ponchartrain, étoufee, and Landry's own delectable sauce make this dining experience a must.

The original Landry's Seafood House, located at 1502 Seawall Blvd, is now **Landry's Oyster Bar on the Seawall.** For great oysters on the half shell, call 409/762-4261. A second location is at Pier 21, 409/762-4747.

## Joe's Crab Shack

3502 Seawall Blvd. • 409/766-1515 • $$–$$$

With seafood the mainstay here, diners enjoy a casual and festive atmosphere with outside seating for viewing passing ships. Employees regularly entertain by jumping on tables and singing their rendition of "YMCA" and other popular songs.

## Fish Tales

2502 Seawall Blvd. • 409/762-8545 • $$–$$$

One of the newest restaurants on Seawall Blvd., the fare is fresh fried, grilled, sautéed, or broiled seafood along with steak and chicken. This multi-level dining establishment, a sister to Fisherman's Wharf, features a fireplace, outdoor decks, two bars, and live music on the weekends.

## Fisherman's Wharf

Pier 22 • 409/765-5708 • $$–$$$

The newly renovated Fisherman's Wharf, on Galveston's port-side, offers indoor and outdoor patio dining with a romantic view of the port. Walk out to the water's edge and see the *Elissa* docked next door to the Texas Seaport Museum. Also in clear view is the 1944 *Ursula M. Norton*, a restored shrimp/clam boat direct from Martha's Vineyard, Massachusetts. The boat has been converted to accommodate guests for lunch and cocktails.

## Casey's Seafood Restaurant

3828 Seawall Blvd. • 409/762-9625 • $$ including salad and drink

The Gaido family also operates Casey's Seafood Restaurant, which offers a casual atmosphere with the same quality food and service as Gaido's. Casey's recently added a patio area with a view of the Gulf for outdoor dining. Seafood, steaks, burgers. The casual atmosphere is perfect for entire family.

## Willie G's Seafood and Steakhouse

Pier 21 2100 Harborside Dr. • 409/762-3030 • $$–$$$

Also known for its delectable seafood fare, Willie G's not only provides quality dining but also offers a serene view of the channel. Many guests choose to stay and enjoy the scenery all night whereas many opt to stroll along the pier to view the Mosquito Fleet nearby or walk to the Strand.

## Hill's Pier 19 Restaurant, Bar, and Fish Market

Pier 19 20th and Harborside Dr. • 409/763-7087 • $–$$

A longtime resident of the port, Hill's is a combination restaurant and market. Visitors may decide to dine here or choose from the display cases of fresh crab, shrimp, and fish, all just off the boats.

# BAKERIES

## The Phoenix Bakery and Coffee House

**2228 Ship's Mechanic Row • 409/763-3764 or 409/763-4611• $–$$$**

For a gourmet continental breakfast or lunch you'll never forget, visit this New Orleans-style bakery with open courtyard that features cappuccino, sandwiches, and fresh pastries baked daily. Try the dilled shrimp salad with cucumbers or the seafood quiche, but save room for dessert. True New Orleans beignets are so light you'll think they were prepared for heavenly bodies. If you like sweet creamy desserts, try the strawberry and melon napoleon. Your diet takes second fiddle to this delectable fare although the menu can accommodate weight-watchers.

# ITALIAN/PIZZA

## DiBella's Italian Restaurant

**1902 31st St. • 409/763-9036 • $$–$$$ • Closed Monday**
**Reservations recommended**

This family owned and operated authentic Italian restaurant offers an intimate setting and a delicious selection of family recipes. The restaurant is extremely popular with Galvestonians and visitors alike. In addition to unforgettable Italian dishes, owner Frank DiBella also serves steaks marinaded in his secret sauce. Lunch and dinner specials.

## Luigi's Italian Restaurant

**2328 Strand • 409/763-6500 • $$–$$$**

Located in the Hutchings-Sealy Building in the Historic Strand District, Luigi's is known for its homemade pasta and delectable shellfish. The "tropical art deco" decor creates an atmosphere that makes dining here all the more memorable.

## Mario's Flying Pizza Restaurant

**2202 61st St. • 628 Seawall Blvd. • 409/744-2975, 409/763-1693 • $$**

Known for its tasty pizza and the show the chef puts on by twirling pizza dough high into the air, Mario's, at two locations, is especially great for families with young kids. A small, no-frills restaurant.

# MEXICAN/SOUTH AMERICAN

## Original Mexican Cafe

1401 Market St. • 409/762-6001 • $–$$

Open for 80 years and an Island favorite, the Original Mexican Cafe (circa 1916) is an institution in the East End Historical District. The original recipes have been passed on from cook to cook over the decades with new dishes being added along the way. Beef enchiladas, tamales, tacos, burritos are all made with lean meats. For breakfast, try Migas Ala Mexicana, a restaurant original, made of fried corn tortillas and eggs and topped with white cheese and mild sauces. Seven different kinds of enchiladas are on the menu.

## Rudy and Paco's

2028 Postoffice St. • 409/762-3696 • $$

Specializes in Nicaraguan dishes. The menu ranges from burgers and chicken and pasta to their house specials such as artichoke ravioli, steak and filet mignon all served with their special chimichurri sauce. As an appetizer, patrons are treated to plantains (fried banana chips). Reservations are recommended as this dining spot draws big crowds.

## El Nopalito Restaurant

6001 Ave. P 1/2 • 409/744-9043 • $$

Owned by the Martinez family, El Nopalito serves up genuine Mexican food from tamales to tacos. If you're a little adventurous and don't mind seeking out those little places hidden among city ruins, plan to have breakfast or lunch at the family's other El Nopalito, located at 614 42nd St. and 6001 Ave. P (409/763-9815). Try their breakfast burritos (served only on weekends) and for lunch, homemade soup and tortillas. The second location is a little hard to find and is only open for breakfast and lunch.

# CONTINENTAL

## The Wentletrap

2301 Strand • 409/765-5545 • $$–$$$$

Chef Dwayne Bosse offers fine dining in an elegantly restored facility.

## The Steakhouse at the San Luis Resort

**5222 Seawall Blvd. • 409/744-1500 • $$–$$$**

The Steakhouse at the San Luis, voted as "best steakhouse on the coast" by *Texas Monthly* magazine, features USDA prime midwest grain-fed steaks as well as seafood, lamb and veal chops, lobster, and red snapper. Gourmet desserts include black forest cake or delectable pecan pie.

## The Merchant Prince

**The Tremont House • 2300 Ship's Mechanic Row • 409/763-0300 $$–$$$$**

Sautéed crab cakes, Gulf quesadillas, grilled flour tortillas with fresh spinach, sautéed mushrooms, lump crab meat and cheese, Oyster Ragout (oysters simmered in a creole brown sauce). Burgers and fries also available as well as non-seafood delicacies such as pineapple chicken.

## Bernardo's

**Hotel Galvez • 2024 Seawall Blvd. • 409/765-7721**

Dine on gourmet continental fare in this luxurious dining room that opens to the historic lobby of the Hotel Galvez.

## The Strand Brewery and Grill

**101 23rd at Harborside Dr. (overlooks Saengerfest Park) • 409/763-4500 $–$$$**

This great brew pub offers four different handcrafted beers along with delicious pastas such as artichoke ravioli; wood-fired tomato and basil pizza; and burgers. You might also consider the restaurant's Thai Roll Ups, made-from-scratch cheesecake, bread pudding with Bourbon sauce, roasted garlic pizza, or baby-back ribs. The food and beer are not the only good thing here. There's a bird's-eye view of the Strand and the harbor from two outdoor decks and the rooftop "biergarten." The three-story restaurant also has pool tables, dart games, and features live music by local artists on Friday and Saturday nights. Music starts around 9 p.m.

## Fitzpatrick's Irish Pub

**2315 Ship's Mechanic Row • 409/765-5914 • $$–$$$**

Another sister property across the street from the hotel, Fitzpatrick's offers a large collection of ales and hearty snack and dinner fare in an Irish pub atmosphere. The Rooftop Terrace offers memorable views of sunrises, sunsets, and ships docking at Galveston's port, with drinks served in the tropical garden.

# Barbecue

## Leon's World's Finest In & Out Barbecue House

101 14th St. • 5427 Broadway • 409/763-5651, 409/744-0070
$–$$

The best in down-home barbecue can be found at Leon's two locations. Some locals call it the "world's finest."

## Queen's Barbecue

3428 Ave. S • 409/762-3151

Another great BBQ place, you'll get your fill of sliced beef here.

# Chinese/Japanese/Vietnamese

## Yamato

2104 61st St. • 409/744-2742 • $$–$$$

Galveston's only Japanese seafood, sushi, and steak house is considered excellent by locals.

## Happy Buddha

2827 61st St. • 409/744-5774 • $–$$$

The offering here is authentic Cantonese and Mandarin cuisine.

## Tin Bo Restaurant

2302 61st St. • 409/740-0990 • $–$$

Offers fine Chinese dining.

## Shanghai Restaurant

2520 Ave. H • 409/762-9384 • $–$$$

Features Vietnamese and Chinese cuisine. Locals say the Vietnamese fare is the better choice here. Located one block from the courthouse.

# NIGHTLIFE

Galveston Island has its share of clubs, over 50 at last count, with many specializing in its share of micro-brews. When there is action, music also rides the sea breezes as blues escape from a brewery to mix with zydeco riding another current. Whether you like the sophistication of hotel surroundings or the intimacy of an English pub, they are all here. However, nightlife, particularly in the Strand district, is low key compared to most seaside cities. Some of the clubs are open only on weekends while others are open everyday to serve lunch and dinner. Hours vary from season to season.

Springfest is celebrated in March by most of the Island's clubs. In addition, all major hotels offer lounges with live entertainment and small dance floors.

## The Strand Brewery and Grill

**101 23rd at Harborside Dr. (overlooks Saengerfest Park)**
**409/763-4500**

The Strand Brewery is a lively brew-pub that offers four different hand-crafted beers along with delicious pastas such as artichoke ravioli, wood-fired tomato and basil pizza, and burgers. You get a bird's-eye view of The Strand and the harbor from two outdoor decks and the rooftop of this hopping "biergarten." Local bands appear regularly on Friday and Saturday nights and play a variety of music from top forty to blues, zydeco, and jazz. Music starts around 9 p.m.

While playing a game of pool or darts, try the beer sampler before deciding on a favorite. Many choose Karankawa Gold as their favorite. The wide variety of German-style beers are brewed on the premises of this three-story restaurant.

## Yaga's Tropical Cafe

2314 Strand • 409/762-6676

This is a favorite among Reggae music lovers. The cafe sponsors the Yaga's Spring Break "Live" during Springfest and spring break. Live bands perform beginning around 10:30 p.m. every Friday and Saturday night. The food includes reasonably priced fare from salads, soups, and sandwiches, to shrimp and chicken entrées. A special break for the health conscious is the lite version of the cafe's main courses.

## Club 42

2314 Strand (upstairs from Yaga's) • 409/762-1100 • Open Thurs.–Sat.

A contemporary nightclub that also sponsors Spring Break Party and Springfest events is patterned to resemble those in L.A. Decor is punctuated by pillars and nineties lighting designed in Italy. Stainless steel bar fronts with gallery-quality photographs add a trendy mood. As for entertainment, this hot spot serves a refined blend of dance music on Saturdays while Fridays are called Disco Ladies' Night. This one is for the college set.

## Parlor Bar

2314 Strand • 409/762-1100 • Open Wed.–Sat.

The Parlor Bar, a quieter appendage of Club 42, is a good place to relax, dance, and gather for late night drinks. The Parlor Bar, which also sponsors events during Springfest and Spring Break, is entered via a brick-paved alley and through 10-ft.-high double doors. Among the cocktails are a menu of martinis and top-shelf drinks. A big hit with all who enter these portals.

## Irish Fitzpatrick's Pub

2315 Ship's Mechanic Row • 409/765-5914 • Open Wed.–Sat.

Pianist Sarah Clayton sets the mood with her renditions at this club housed in one of the oldest buildings in Galveston. Big band and swing favorites are also favorites at this true Irish pub. Fitzpatrick's, another sister property across the street from the hotel, offers a large collection of ales and hearty snack and dinner fare that appeals to a mixed crowd. The Rooftop Terrace offers memorable views of sunrises, sunsets, and ships docking at Galveston's port.

## Henry Toujouse Bar
## The Tremont House
### 2300 Ship's Mechanic Row • 409/763-0300 ext. 550

The Henry Toujouse Bar, located in the atrium of the Tremont House, features a beautiful rosewood bar that dates back to 1872 when a young Frenchman by the name of Henry Toujouse found work at the Opera House Saloon. At that time the saloon was located in the basement of the Tremont Opera House at Tremont and Market.

When the owner died, Toujouse took over the saloon business and managed it until the opera house was sold in 1894. He then moved across Tremont St., opening first Henry's Cafe, then the Stag Hotel. He took with him this elaborately ornamented bar. In 1913, Henry Toujouse sold his hotel and retired. The bar disappeared, until in the 1960s, it was found, purchased, and later donated to the Galveston Historical Foundation. Today, it is leased from the foundation and has been restored to its original beauty.

## O'Malley's Stage Door Pub
### 2022 Postoffice St. • 409/763-1731

This old Irish pub features live acoustic rock entertainment with happy hour from 3–7 p.m. The atmosphere is casual, and if you're hungry, ownership serves deli sandwiches. More than 100 imported bottled beers. Cigars available.

## Molly's Pub
### 2013 Postoffice St. • 409/763-4466

Molly's Pub is an authentic Irish pub serving more than 60 draft beers. Cigars. Open daily.

## The Galveston Brewery
### 2521 Ship's Mechanic Row • 409/763-3484 • Food served on weekdays only

Galveston's second microbrewery, housed in one of the original cotton gins of early 1900, offers its own brew as well as domestic and foreign beers. The brewery includes a game room and offers sandwiches. The music here is lively and varies from blues to jazz to alternative.

## Club Galvez

### 2024 Seawall Blvd. • 409/765-7721

Club Galvez is a popular venue for live entertainment, as guests dance to the sounds of popular local entertainers Friday and Saturday evenings. Appetizers, sandwiches, and salads are served at this posh Hotel Galvez night spot. The surroundings are antique mahogany with brass trim and very elegant.

## Todd's on the Strand

### 2120 Strand • 409/765-8606

A combination cafe and club, Todd's is located in the heart of the Strand. Outdoor tables give one an unobstructed view of the bustling street, and at Christmas the place is decorated with lights and a huge Christmas tree at the entrance. The food at this casual club varies from hamburgers to seafood baskets and platters. Kids are welcome.

## Old Cellar Door

### 2015 Postoffice St. • 409/763-4477

A unique antique bar, serving brandies, scotches, and wines. Cigars. Open daily.

## Nina's Bourbon Street West

### 215 22nd St. between Strand and Mechanic streets • 409/762-8894

If you like New Orleans, you'll love Nina's, a jazzy club with nonstop entertainment. Listen to the blues while you choose a beer from the 60 domestic and imported varieties, as well as mixed drinks and wine. If you like to dance, there is a dance floor in the back. The appetizer menu includes Cajun wings, of course, and a New Orleans-style muffuletta—a 9-in.-round bread sandwich of meats, and cheeses topped with an olive-based relish. The favorite among customers, though, is Nina's "white pizza," a pie of spinach fettuccine.

## The Old Quarter Acoustic Cafe

### 413 20th St. • 409/762-9199 • Open Tues.–Sat. evenings

Music is the main fare with acoustic, country, or alternative bands. A popular spot among locals.

## The Press Box Cafe and Club

**2401 Postoffice St. • 409/765-5958**

A sports bar that serves food.

## The Veranda

**Hotel Galvez • 2024 Seawall Blvd. • 409/765-7721**

A romantic spot in an historic hotel for drinks and light fare.

## Balinese Room

**21st St. and Seawall Blvd.**

At this writing, the legendary Balinese Room has just been purchased by real estate investor Bob Greig, who plans to open a dinner and dance club on the familiar long pier extending over the Gulf of Mexico. Located across from the Hotel Galvez, the club was once owned by gambling king-pins Sam and Rose Maceo. A favorite among movie stars, oil barons, gang-sters, and gamblers, the Balinese Room, built in the 1920s, was a fashion-able restaurant and nightclub, and was known for its illegal casino operations until reformers closed its doors. Ever-present on the Galveston scene, the vacant structure is now under renovation and slated to open in the summer of 1998.

# BOLIVAR PENINSULA

## Bolivar Peninsula Chamber of Commerce

1760 Hwy. 87 • P.O. Box 1170 • Crystal Beach, TX 77650
409/684-5940, 800 FUN-SUN 3 • http://www.bolivar.com,
http://www.crystalbeach.com

Formed 5,000 years ago by the forces of nature, the Bolivar Peninsula, a narrow strip of land separated from Galveston Island by less than three miles of water, is a long sandy stretch with sporadic sprouting of weathered beachhouses and campy little sea retreats. The 27-mile long peninsula gives no-frills beachlovers a chance to be private, you can fish without getting your line tangled with other fishermen, and quietly watch as distant tankers carry oil back and forth along the coast. Encompassing beach communities include Port Bolivar, Crystal Beach, Caplen, Gilchrist, and High Island. The area is also a stopping place for birds traveling elsewhere for the winter. There are some good eating places here, too, and for overnighters, rental cottages abound if you know who to contact.

The summer, particularly in August, is not a great burst of color but for the naturalist there is true beauty here in the small patches of wildflowers. Subtle bloomings are hidden among the swamp grasses, scrub brush, passion flower, Japanese honeysuckle, prickly pear cactus, and sand dunes. Red and yellow Indian blankets, lavender butterfly pea vines, pink powder puffs, red Turk's cap, black-eyed Susans, morning glories, giant sunflowers and coreopsis add splashes of color under an open sky seagulls call home.

Here, on this thirty-mile long sandy strip, which separates the Gulf of Mexico from intercoastal canal and East Galveston Bay waters, vacationers find many spots to crab—off bridges, on crags that border inlets, and in the surf (use a sand-filled plastic milk bottle) to anchor your bait. Fishermen also have many places to cast their lines. **Rollover Pass**, located down the peninsula about 20 minutes away, is a man-made cut that connects the bay to the surf.

Visit the Bolivar Peninsula by taking the free Bolivar-Galveston Ferry ride.

# BOLIVAR PENINSULA

GALVESTON BAY

Galveston Bolivar Ferry Landing

PORT BOLIVAR

108

87

CRYSTAL BEACH

Unrestricted Beach Access

Crystal Beach Rd.

Kahla Rd.

Bay Vue Dr.

Sandpiper

Stingaree Cove

INTRACOASTAL WATERWAY

EAST BAY

Sandy Castle Dr.

87

CAPLIN

GILCHRIST

to Anahuac & High Island

Rollover Pass

GULF OF MEXICO

N

# BOLIVAR HISTORY AND FORT TRAVIS

In 1816, Frances Xavier Mina, while on a Spanish expedition for Spain, constructed an earthen levee to protect himself and his men from the Karankawa Indians on what is today the Fort Travis Seashore Park, a beachfront picnic ground and campground with oleanders, palm trees, and black-eyed susans.

Dr. James Long and approximately 300 troops, came to Texas to liberate it from Spanish rule. Long's 19-year-old wife, Jane, a Natchez beauty, found herself in Bolivar's crude Fort Travis in August 1919 while her husband tried without success to secure the services of Jean Lafitte who occupied Galveston Island at the time. Long, ordered to leave on expedition to capture Presidio La Bahia, again left Jane, one of their children, and a servant at the fort with only a handful of men to protect them. The winter of 1821 was bitterly cold and the men, ordered to protect them, decided to desert. To trick Lafitte's pirates into thinking the fort was still defended, Jane fired a cannon every morning. She didn't know, however, what enemy to fear most—the Spaniards, Mexicans, Lafitte and his pirates, or the Karankawa Indians. During the winter of 1820-21, Mrs. Long, 20-years-old, gave birth to the first white child born in Texas, a girl. The baby was delivered by Jane herself in a raging December storm as her servant was delirious with a fever. The baby was named Mary and was the first baby of English descent to be born in Texas. Known as "the Mother of Texas," the heroic Mrs. Long remained at the fort until 1822 when she received word that her husband, Dr. Long, had been killed. She later ran a boarding house in Richmond.

## Crystal Beach

**Hwy. 87**

Proceeding east on Highway 87, you'll come to Crystal Beach, a salty little beach community, famous for its watermelon crop. The largest of these small hamlets, Crystal Beach, advertises plane rides, horseback riding, a water slide, and a beachside golf course. Once famous for growing watermelons, it has a sprinkling of restaurants, motels, an RV park and page after page of rental properties. Los Patos, a fishing and hunting club, is also in residence here. The principal industry is shrimping and oystering, with retail sales available to the public. Also there is one full-time doctor and clinic facilities available for emergencies, but you may want to bring a first aid kit.

## Gilchrist and Rollover Pass

**Hwy. 87**

Located in the small seaside town of Gilchrist, Rollover, the narrowest part of the peninsula about 20 minutes northeast of the ferry landing, is a cut where the Gulf and the bay meet. According to local historians, Rollover was called this because in early days, pirates and ship captains who wanted to avoid Galveston customs officials, unloaded their barrels of Jamaican Rum and other imported merchandise near shore. They rolled the barrels over to East Bay where they were transported to the mainland. The Fish Pass, opened in 1955 by the Texas Game and Fish Commission, is a channel about 1,600 feet long across the peninsula from the Gulf to East Bay. The purpose was to add salinity to the bay and thus increase the salt-water fish. The cut, which is smothering local oyster reefs and causing some beach erosion, has greatly improved salt-water fishing here and is a very popular spot for fisherman, as a result.

As for Gilchrist, its history revolves around the day when "the Gilchrist Post Office rolled away." The story stems from 1964 when Hurricane Hilda threatened the upper Texas coast. The postmaster, who owned the building and rented it to the postal department, was so worried he would lose his property, that he hoisted it on wheels and hauled it to High Island. When Gilchrist residents went there to retrieve their mail, they saw a sign on the side of the building. It read, "The mail must go on." When the hurricane changed courses and hit Louisiana instead, he rolled it back to Gilchrist. From then on the postmaster left the post office on wheels in case another hurricane decided to slam into the peninsula.

## High Island

### Hwy. 87 and Hwy. 124

High Island is formerly known as Doe Island by the Indians. If you're interested in geological formations and Texas history, turn inland on Hwy. 124 and drive to High Island, named for its elevation. The 47-ft. salt dome is the highest point on the island between Port Bolivar and Sabine Pass. Note the colorful stand of oleanders on the left side of the highway. This was once the site of the 1895 Sea View Hotel, a large ornate luxury accommodation open to summer visitors who would arrive by an excursion train. All that is left of the Sea View is its iron fence. The hotel offered fine food, boasted a beautiful ballroom, and supplied "nannies" to care for children when adults went dancing. There was also a mule-drawn rail car to transport guests to the beachside. In 1947, the facility burned to the ground.

Drive to 5th St., pass the unmarked post office, and go to the High Island Cemetery. Charles A. Cronea, possibly the last crew member of Jean Lafitte's band of pirates, is buried there. Known as "Uncle Charlie" to the children of High Island, he was born in Marseille, France, in 1805. In 1818, he set sail to America on a French frigate as its cabin boy. Unhappy with the dozen whip lashes he received, he deserted the frigate in the New York harbor in 1819. Later, he signed on for a cruise to the Gulf of Mexico. He went ashore near Corpus Christi where he signed on as cabin boy with a brig—its captain, Jean Lafitte. When he was forced to stand on the breech of the pivot gun for half an hour for spilling water on Captain James Campbell, Lafitte's right hand man, he vowed to jump ship when they reached Louisiana. Later he moved to High Island in 1875 where he met Henry Sullivan, who later became his son-in-law. Sullivan's home is still standing in the town.

If you want to visit Cronea's grave, who was also a veteran of the Battle of San Jacinto and the Mexican War, and a Texas pioneer, look for a grave capped by beach shells and concrete. The headstone is cracked and bears only "Charles A . . ." Further north and east into High Island is the site of the famous mineral spring, which was said to be a hot spring. This spring was visited by thousands when the railroad was in operation. The sulfurous water was thought to have curative powers. People bathed in it and drank its water. Located on now obscure land called "the old Grandma Smith Estate," the site is very popular with bird watchers. The old buildings have fallen, the gardens are overgrown, but it's very peaceful and secluded. Oaks and crepe myrtles, planted in 1875, share residence with flocks of birds.

Beyond the intersection of Hwy. 87 and Hwy. 124, the road is closed. Once a scenic stretch along the coastline that led to Sabine Pass and then Port Arthur, it is now unpassable, barracked because of storm damage.

## ATTRACTIONS

### The Galveston-Bolivar Ferry

Ferry Rd. (State Hwy. 87) • Galveston Ferry Operations Department of Highways and Public Transportation • P.O. Box 381 • Galveston, TX 77553-0381 • 409/763-2386 • Free

Launched in 1930, the Galveston-Bolivar Ferry system, now with six ferries leaving every 20 minutes, takes visitors from Galveston Island to the narrow 27-mile-long Bolivar Peninsula. Seagulls escort the vessels as they shuttle visitors, residents, and sportsmen back and forth through waters once sailed by Jean Lafitte, and dolphins often race the 588-ton ferries on this three-mile crossing. Ocean-going ships may be seen on their way to and from the wharves at Galveston, Texas City, or Houston.

If you'll look to the left, you'll see a large concrete structure sticking out of the water, which is the remains of a concrete ship, *Selma*. She was built as one of 12 experimental vessels built by the United States during WWI. Before the ship could ever see action, however, the strapping 6,000-ton vessel sank in 1922. Passing seagoers can see the ship's ghostly hull, still intact, sticking half out of the water.

Bring your camera as there is much to shoot on this enchanting ride. The observation deck gives one a panoramic view of this gull's way. Bring along old bread to feed the seagulls; however, unless you want your summer whites soiled, be sure to do so at the stern. Also, gulls at the bow obstruct the captain's vision.

A note of caution—during peak seasons, the wait is quite long. In that case, if you just want the ride and have no plans to explore the peninsula, drive up to the ferry dock, park your car, and walk on-board. While on your trip, watch for brown pelicans and notice the historic Port Bolivar

Lighthouse, built in 1872, as you deboard. It is located about one mile from the Bolivar Ferry pier on Bolivar Peninsula.

## The Bolivar Lighthouse

**Privately owned; not open to the public • One mile down Hwy. 87**

The Bolivar Lighthouse, constructed in 1872, is the second of its kind located here. The first was constructed in 1852 of cast-iron and was torn down by the Confederates during the Civil War for wartime material. Marking the entrance to Galveston Harbor, its concrete and brick tower, encased in solid riveted sheet tin, rises 117 feet from its base and acts as a familiar landmark for residents and visitors. The top of the tower, which once housed the revolving lamp, is built of steel and iron.

For 61 years, the 52,000-candle-power beacon flashed across the waters of the Gulf, guiding ships safely into Galveston Harbor. Its beacon could be seen from 50 miles out. A survivor of the 1900 Storm, it provided safe haven for 125 people. Harry C. Claiborne, lighthouse keeper, fed the storm survivors until his own food supply was exhausted. The Sept. 8th hurricane sent winds so strong it caused the tower to sway so badly the machinery for the light wouldn't work. That night, Mr. Claiborne rotated the machinery by hand and kept the beacon bright.

The later 1915 Storm took away all the kerosene oil, leaving only two gallons of fuel to keep its light burning. The sea rose until its base, 11 feet above sea level, was shoulder deep in water. During that storm, 61 people found protection here, huddling on the circular stairs as 175 mph winds roared around the lighthouse. For the first time in history, its light did not shine for two days.

In 1990, the lighthouse was retired. The inner mechanisms have been removed and the lamps and reflector lenses have been reassembled in the Galveston County Museum. It was the setting for the 1968 movie, *My Sweet Charlie*, with Patty Duke and Al Freeman, Jr. Because the lighthouse is privately owned, visitors are not allowed.

## Fort Travis Seashore Park

**Galveston County Beach Park Board • 601 Tremont, Suite 100 Galveston, TX 77550 • 409/766-2411 • Park Hours: Gates locked between dark and 7:30 a.m. • Check-in time: 9 a.m.–7 p.m.; check out by 11 a.m.**

Now 60 acres, the park was acquired through a Moody Foundation grant of $200,000 in March 1976. Coupled with a development grant from the National Park Service, it is now the Fort Travis Seashore Park.

The U.S. began a seacoast fortification program in 1888, the first major defense expenditure undertaken since the end of the Civil War. Three forts were built in the Galveston Bay area between 1897 and 1899. During WWI, Fort Travis was used as a garrison for troops defending the Galveston coastal waters and the vital Port of Galveston. In 1942, Fort Travis was enlarged to accommodate 2,500 troops to provide area defenses.

The park provides cabana rentals, campsites, and picnic areas. To date, there are six cabanas which rent at $15 per night. Each contains a small picnic table, sink, and electrical outlets. There are larger picnic tables and grills outside the cabanas. Showers and restrooms are located nearby. Advanced reservations are accepted in writing or by phone. Occupancy of cabanas or campsites by the same person or group is limited to 7 consecutive calendar days. Campsites are $10 per night per unit. Camping permits are required. Advanced reservations are not required but are available from the Galveston County Beach Park Board. Information on organized group camping rates can also be obtained. A maximum of eight persons and two vehicles are permitted per site. Showers and restrooms are located nearby. Beer is allowed in park but no wine or liquor. Campfires in grills only. Fireworks and firearms are prohibited. Persons under 18 years of age may stay overnight only if accompanied by parent or legal guardian or with written permission.

Vehicles must remain on designated roadways or parking areas only. Picnic sites, shelters, picnic tables, and cooking grills are located throughout the park and are available on a first- come basis. Park visitors have access to sandy beaches where they can fish for flounder, trout, and red drum. There is also a playground. To get there, take State Hwy. 87 to Crystal Beach and watch for the park sign. Along the way you'll pass cattle on open ranges, signs pointing to fish camps, shrimp, crab and oyster plants, and a few weather beaten retail stores, many of which offer fresh seafood.

## Shrimp Fleet

Just as you drive off the ferry on the Bolivar side, turn inland on Loop 108 and cut through the town of Port Bolivar. When you approach Spur 108 as it dead ends, you'll be able to see, up close, a tiny fleet of commercial shrimp boats and seafood-packing plants.

## The North Jetty

Off Hwy. 87, about ¼ mile from the fort is North Jetty Rd. Unmarked except for a large sign on the inland side of the highway, the road dead ends into the North Jetty, one of two jetties that protect the entrance to the ship channel. Built of huge granite blocks in the 1890s by the Army Corp of Engineers, the structures, which keep back silt that would make the area unnavigatible, allow ships to travel the channel. The North Jetty extends five miles into the Gulf. Visitors may walk two miles out on the jetty to see how the fish are biting. This is a favorite spot among anglers.

## Beachcombing

Walk along this quiet 30-mile stretch of beach and find seashells, sand dollars, driftwood, and sea beans. Two rustic stables on the peninsula provide horses for inland and beach riding. Almost deserted beaches provide privacy with nature. The wind, generally off the Gulf, provides for catamarans, sail boards, and limited surfing.

## Sea Rim State Park

P.O. Box 1066 • Sabine Pass, TX 77655 • 409/971-2559 • $2 per vehicle • Open daily except certain days during migratory waterfowl season when part of the park is closed

Sea Rim Park, a 15,000-acre coastal marshland, stretches a sandy 5½ miles along the ocean. Ten miles west of Sabine Pass on State Hwy. 87, this part of the peninsula is considered Jefferson County. A bird lover's paradise in the spring, this state facility provides the tourist quiet seclusion from city life. It was purchased by Planet Oil and Mineral Corporation and Horizon Corporation to preserve coastal estuaries and wetlands. There are also boat trails and boardwalks into the marshland. It is named for that portion of the Gulf shoreline where the marsh grasses extend into the surf in a zone termed sea rim marsh—an estuarine system important for its abundance of furbearers and waterfowl.

The kids love the observation deck and the wildlife museum on the second floor. There, visitors learn about egrets, spoonbills, alligators, sea turtles, and the red-tail hawk. Your family will leave knowing much more about the Gulf waters, home of over 400 species of fish. To see wildlife, take the Gambusia Nature Trail, a 7⁄10-mile boardwalk into the marsh. Wading birds as well as nutria, mink, raccoon, rabbit, skunk, opossum, the American alligator, river otters, ducks, geese, and other waterfowl call this home. Be forewarned, however. An alligator, who lives near the path, craves hamburgers and hot dogs. You had better leave lunch back at park headquarters, located next to to the museum.

Along the park beach, no traffic is allowed, but there is ample parking at headquarters. Visitors may camp along the shore or in the designated camping area, which contains 20 RV sites equipped with water, electrical hookups, and a sewage dump station. In the Marshlands Unit, a boat ramp, boat channel, and pirogue/canoe trails give access into the marsh. The visitor may fish or crab, camp on one of the six camping platforms, or observe and photograph wildlife from one of the observation blinds.

## Sabine Pass Battleground State Historical Park

1½ miles south of the city of Sabine Pass on Farm Rd. 3322, and 15 miles south of Port Arthur via Hwy. 87.

If you're a Civil War buff, travel another 12 miles to Sabine Pass for a visit to the 56-acre Sabine Pass Battleground State Historical Park. It is located along the Sabine River Ship Channel on the site of Fort Sabine (also known as Fort Griffin), which was built during the Civil War to guard the river from Union invasion forces. Here, Lieutenant Dick Dowling and 46 men defeated and repelled 22 Union gunboats in this notable battle. The Dick Dowling Days Festival is held each year on Labor Day weekend to commemorate the Sept. 8, 1863 battle. Visitors may also fish or crab off the bank, but beware of passing tall ships that send waves onto the land where anglers usually stand.

# Texas Crab Festival

Bolivar Peninsula Chamber of Commerce • 409/684-5940
Annual May Festival/Mother's Day Weekend • Admission:
$3 per person, under 12 free

The Texas Crab Festival is a folksy event that celebrates the Gulf Coast crab. There are food and craft booths and a crab cook-off in the carnival-like atmosphere. Live entertainment, and dancing under a covered tent ends each day of crab races, crab leg contests, and volleyball tournaments. Bring lawn chairs. No food or drinks can be brought into festival grounds.

# Anahuac National Wildlife Refuge

P.O. Box 278 • Anahuac, TX 77514 • 409/267-3337 • (Refuge headquarters is on corner of Trinity and Washington streets near the Anahuac County Courthouse.)

Located west of Sabine Pass, the Anahuac National Wildlife Refuge is another birdwatcher's favorite. The refuge contains 24,293 acres of marsh-land, which is a winter habitat for ducks and geese of the Central Flyway. Anahuac is an important link in the chain of refuges extending southward along the Texas Gulf Coast. The refuge more than doubled in size in 1982 with the acquisition of the Anahuac Public Hunting Area. Federal duck stamp revenues provided funds for the acquisition of the refuge.

The brackish marsh and wet prairie communities see as many as 20 kinds of ducks and four species of geese. Snow geese, sometimes in excess of 50,000, rest here to be close to the rice fields. Anahuac is also a prime nesting area for the mottled duck, a year-round resident of the Texas coast. Visitors also see herons, egrets, and ibis, as well as furbearers, the muskrat, and the nutria. The raccoon, opossum, mink, skunk, bobcat, and river otter also reside here.

The winter and spring months are best for birdwatching, particularly around Shoveler Pond and Teal Slough. There are no photography blinds, but you can get a special permit to erect a temporary one. There are 12 miles of graveled roads, which can accommodate buses and recreational vehicles, although they are not suitable for biking. Visitors should tank up before entering the preserve, as there are no gas stations. Off-road travel is prohibited. Firearms are unlawful except in designated areas during hunting season.

You may walk anywhere, but there are no developed hiking trails. If you choose to walk along the levees, watch for poisonous snakes, fire ants, and alligators. Bring insect repellent to ward off mosquitoes. Restroom facilities are at the refuge entrance and at two locations on East Galveston Bay. Bring your own drinking water.

Fishing and boating are permitted only in East Galveston Bay, bayous, and other locations designated by refuge signs. There are no developed boat ramps on the refuge and boats will encounter shallow water conditions. The best location for canoeing is Oyster Bayou. Hunting is permitted during hunting season at the Anahuac Public Hunting Area—located seven miles east of the main refuge on FM 1985. Hunters should contact refuge headquarters in the fall before waterfowl season to obtain hunting regulations and permits.

Camping is permitted only along the shore of East Galveston Bay and is limited to three days. No camping facilities are provided, as camping is not encouraged. The nearest camping facilities are at Fort Anahuac Park and White Memorial Park north of Anahuac along I-10. Motel accommodations are available in Anahuac, Winnie, and High Island.

## Bolivar Flats Shorebird Sanctuary

If you like birdwatching, this sanctuary is an important resting and feeding location for migrating shorebirds from throughout the Western Hemisphere. Here, in the marshes, reddish egrets, roseate spoonbill, snow geese, ospreys, Cooper's hawks, merlins, short-eared owls, belted kingfishers, eastern meadowlarks, solitary sandpipers, and Bonaparte's gull, come to nest. At first glance, you may not suspect the special qualities of Bolivar Flats, a unique area combining salt march, mud flats, and beach, each habitat quite different from the other.

The 5-mile long North Jetty, built by the U.S. Corps of Engineers and completed in 1898, is the reason thousands of birds feed, rest, and build nests. Built to protect the mouth of Galveston Bay, the jetty diverts the currents that parallel the coast causing sediments to drop to the bottom. Bolivar Flats Shorebird Sanctuary consists of 550 acres of salt marsh, beach, and uplands that were created as these sediments accumulated.

Funded by the U.S. Fish and Wildlife Service, Phillips Petroleum Company, and the Houston Audubon Society.

## Boy Scout Woods and Smith Oaks
## Houston Audubon Society Nature Sanctuaries

High Island, TX • Houston Audubon Society Office at Edith L. Moore Nature Sanctuary: 713/932-1639 • Lone Star Rare Bird Alert: 713/992-2757

These are two small but very important bird sanctuaries on Bolivar's High Island located only a mile from the beach. They act as a meeting ground for the annual trans-Gulf migration of birds moving north after a winter in the warm climates of South and Central America. In early March, when millions of songbirds push north to the Yucatan Peninsula and the adjacent Mexican coast to establish territories and find mates, this spot becomes a chorus of calls from birds representing 30 migrant species.

Spring also brings wood warblers, tanagers, orioles, and other neo-tropical migrants. Others come in waves as cold fronts or spring thunderstorms make traveling difficult. When wet, exhausted birds seek shelter, they come and land in huge flocks—called a "fallout." Boy Scout Woods and Smith Oaks, located on the salt dome at High Island, stand out as the only substantial feature above the surrounding marshlands for more than 10 miles in any direction. During a fallout, these two sanctuaries, combining to encompass 24 acres, also are home for most resident species of the eastern North American forest ecosystem. No camping, but restrooms and drinkable water available. To witness spring migration, visit from mid-March to mid-May. In the fall, visit from August through October.

To get there, continue on Hwy. 87, then left on Hwy. 124 to enter High Island. At the post office, turn right and go east on 5th St. about ¼ mile, and you're there.

### Boat Parade at Stingaree during Christmas
409/864-2731

The second weekend in December local boat owners decorate their boats and parade along Stingaree Marina and Restaurant at Crystal Beach in celebration of the season. Call 409/684-2731.

# ACCOMMODATIONS

## RENTALS

### Beach House Sales and Rentals
Cobb Real Estate • Hwy. 87 at Sandpiper • P.O. Box 1429
Crystal Beach, TX 77650 • 409/684-3790, 800/880-2622

### Swede's Beach Property
Hwy. 87 • P.O. Box 1158 • Crystal Beach, TX 77650
409/684-3345, 800/624-0071

### Hamilton Real Estate
Hwy. 87 • P.O. Box 1633 • Crystal Beach, TX 77650
409/694-3792, 800/684-3792

# Motels

### Gulfway Motel and Restaurant
Hwy. 124 • P.O. Box 307 • High Island, TX 77623 • 409/286-5217

### Crystal Palace Resort
1600 Hwy. 87 • P.O. Box 2040 • Crystal Beach, TX 77650
409/684-6554, 800/284-6554

### Joy Sands Motel
1020 Hwy. 87 • P. O. Box 1226 • Crystal Beach, TX 77650
409/684-6152

### Fisherman's Cove Motel
Hwy. 87 • P.O. Box 575 • Port Bolivar, TX 77650 • 409/864-8567

### Martha's Vineyard Guest House
962 Martha's Vineyard • P.O. Box 22 • Gilchrist, TX 77617
409/286-5441

# Lodges

### Los Patos
Hunting and Fishing Lodge • 939 Los Patos Dr. • Gilchrist, TX 77617
409/286-5767, 281/852-6456

Los Patos is a lodge open primarily as a private facility but owners do some bookings for non-members. The facility is located on the beach and accommodates up to 30. Restaurants are nearby for meals. Fishing spots here are convenient. During hunting season, prime duck and goose hunts with 13,000 acres of private marsh are available. Owners also have 50,000 acres under private lease.

# RV Parks

### Quality Bait and RV Park
Hwy. 87 • P.O. Box 68 • Gilchrist, TX 77617-0068 • 409/286-5712

## Way Out Marina

1228 North Redfish Dr. • P.O. Box 1493 • Crystal Beach, TX 77650
409/684-3070

## Beachbuster R.V. Park and Bar

1755 Hwy. 87 • P.O. Box 1649 • Crystal Beach, TX 77650
409/684-4929, 409/684-5929

# PENINSULA RESTAURANTS

Although the peninsula lacks the elegant restaurants of Gaido's or the many other dining places found along Galveston's scenic Seawall and the historic Strand District, you can eat like royalty if you know where to go.

## Stringaree Restaurant and Marina

1295 Stingaree Rd. • P.O. Box 1410 • Crystal Beach, TX 77650
409/684-2731

A favorite among the family-owned weathered restaurants is George Vratis' Stingaree Restaurant (Crystal Beach), which specializes in fresh seafood. If you're a big eater, you must try the "all-you-can-eat" ($18.95/person) gastronomic feast that features endless supplies of barbecued, fried, and boiled crabs. Vratis also specializes in soft shell almondine ($14.95), a crab delight with meuniere sauce and almond butter. The fried shrimp plate ($9.95) is also a favorite. If it's crawfish season, try the crawfish boudreaux, a spicy tomato-crawfish stew served over linguine.

The marina next door is owned and operated by George's brother Bosco. If the restaurant is crowded, which is a given during peak hours, stroll over to the marina and soak in the view of seagulls and calm bay water. To get there, take Hwy. 87 off the ferry and head down to Crystal Beach. Look for the Stingaree sign on the left. The restaurant and marina are located on the bay side of the peninsula.

## Bolivar Landing Restaurant

2283 Hwy. 87 • P.O. Box 327 • Gilchrist, TX 77617 • 409/286-5449

## Decoux's Pub and Restaurant

3150 Hwy. 87 • P.O. Box 1633 • Crystal Beach, TX 77650
409/684-0177

## Sartin's Seafood

2590 Hwy. 87 • General Delivery • Crystal Beach, TX 77650
409/684-8646

# BAIT AND FRESH SEAFOOD

## Seafood and Fishing
Milt's Seafood • 1414 7ᵗʰ St. • Bolivar, Tx 77650 • 409/684-6464

## Rollover Pass Bait and Tackle
South side of the pass • 409/286-5562

## Bait House
Rollover Bait and Tackle • 409/286-5562

## Granny's Bait Camp
Rollover Pass • Gilchrist, Tx 77617 • 409/286-5702

# MEDICAL

## Crystal Beach Medical Center
Fire House Building • 1698 Hwy. 87 (10.7 miles from ferry landing)
P.O. Box 1421 • Crystal Beach 77650 • 409/684-6702 • Mon.–Fri.
8 a.m.–5 p.m., Sat. 9 a.m.–12 p.m.

# Clear Lake/NASA Area

## Clear Lake/NASA Area Convention and Visitors Bureau
1201 NASA Road 1 • Houston, TX 77058-3391 • 281/488-7676
or 800/844-LAKE

## Attractions, Tours, and Points of Interest

### NASA/Johnson Space Center
### Space Center Houston (official visitors center)
1601 NASA Rd. 1 • Houston, TX 77058 • 281/244-2100,
800/972-0369 • Mon.–Fri. 10 a.m.–5 p.m. • Sat.–Sun. 10 a.m.–7 p.m.
Summer hours (Memorial Day–Labor Day) daily 9 a.m.–7 p.m.
Adults $13, seniors $12, children (4-11) $9 • Wheelchair accessible
and wheelchairs available to rent at front gate

Located between Galveston and Houston on NASA Rd. 1 off I-45, this is
a "behind the scenes" look at NASA's heart. The Johnson Space Center
houses the National Aeronautics and Space Administration complex and the
Space Shuttle Orbiter Training Building and the Lunar Sample Building.

**NASA Tram Tour.** A tram takes guests on a tour of Johnson Space Center
where they can witness the Weightless Environment Training Facility; the
Control Center Complex with the new Space Station Control Center,
areas where astronauts train in simulated environments; and Rocket Park,
the outdoor home of enormous, retired flight hardware.

**Space Center Houston.** The biggest attraction, designed by Walt Disney
engineers, is Space Center Houston, the new visitors center. Exhibitions
here, built around the magic of imagineering, take visitors through the his-

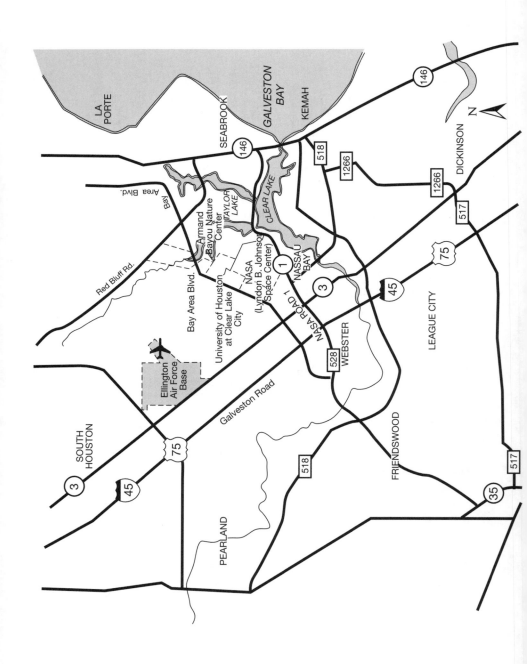

tory of NASA's Manned Space Program. Interactive exhibits work with giant IMAX screens to submerge visitors in simulated experiences where they can interact with real astronauts and see the latest in technological advancements. You'll see a mock-up of the space shuttle just as you enter the Plaza.

**Kids Space Place**, also a new edition, gives kids a chance to learn about space exploration and the basic math and science concepts required for the expeditions through 17 different interactive play areas. At the Mission Status Center, you'll have the chance to listen in on communications between Mission Control and astronaut crews on board the space shuttle. The Feel of Space exhibits allow visitors to interact with 24 computer simulators that allow them to try to land the shuttle or retrieve a satellite.

To facilitate your visit, ask NASA to send a packet of information along with a map of the center. This way you and your family can decide what needs to be covered and how much time will be needed to see it. The earlier you arrive, the better chance you have to avoid the crowds. The NASA cafeteria (The Zero-G Diner) offers a variety of food from hamburgers to salads.

**Astronaut Gallery.** See actual space suits worn by America's space explorers such as Alan Shepard's silvery suit, created for the high-G blastoff during the Mercury program and Dick Covey's Hawaiian shirt worn on the Space Shuttle. Learn about the different types of suits in the astronaut wardrobe depending upon the job they are doing.

**Neutral Buoyancy Lab.** Neutral Buoyancy Lab uses the largest indoor pool in the U.S. to simulate the zero gravity environment of space through the effect of "neutral buoyancy." The 102-ft. wide by 202 ft.-long and 40 ft.-deep pool contains 6.2 million gallons of water.

**Destiny Theater.** This gallery recounts the great moments of space program in the 15-minute film, "On Human Destiny." Through historic footage and historical space artifacts, you get a real sense of man's vast advancements in the field of space travel. Hardware includes the *Gemini 5* spacecraft, a Lunar Roving Vehicle trainer, the *Apollo 17* command module, and the Skylab Trainer. Also here is the world's largest display of Moon rocks as well as feature films shown on a giant IMAX screen that rotates.

## Annual Ballunar Liftoff Festival

Johnson Space Center/NASA Clear Lake Chamber of Commerce
281/488-7676 or 800/844-LAKE for parking/shuttle information • Late
August • $2 per person, under 12 free • Cost covers round-trip shuttle
Shuttles leave from I-45 at Baybrook Mall's south parking lot or
METRO's Bay Area Blvd. • Gates open 6 p.m. Fri., Sat., Sun.

Now a permanent stop on the U.S. balloon tour circuit, the Annual Ballunar Liftoff Festival celebrates the oldest form of human flight with the most modern form—today's space vehicles. Throughout the day, hundreds of brilliantly colored balloons take off from the festival, a breathtaking sight that appeals to the sense of adventure in all of us.

The event also features live bands, midway rides, demonstrations of miniature aircraft, including model airplanes and radio-controlled planes. Also highlighting Saturday's activities is an Open House at the Johnson Space Center where the public is invited to go behind the scenes in a tour of NASA's astronaut training facilities, space vehicle mock-ups, and other areas. On Saturday night, festival activities include the UFO Invasion and a Balloon Glow of specialty-shaped balloons. The evening's colorful mass ascension of hot air balloons is set usually for around 6 p.m. A final launch for the weekend is usually scheduled for Sunday evening about 6 p.m. Call for verification of times as they tend to change from year to year. Also, the Great American Skydiving Competition puts on a show on both Saturday and Sunday. Three 40-member teams of All-American skydivers (expert level), with each team in red, white, and blue, build multiple formations in the sky. In an unparalleled pyrotechnic show, the Elvises of the Sky skydive.

Other attractions include hang gliders, music, arts and crafts booths, rides and games for the kids, food and beverages, commercial exhibits, Confederate Air Force flyovers, model rocket launchings, radio-controlled aircraft, and the Ballunar Liftoff's premier balloon—the Nassau Bay Texas Space Shuttle Balloon, so big it was tested inside the Houston Astrodome. Sightseers in the past have seen balloons in the shapes of giant hamburgers, a tennis shoe, a hot dog, a fish, a whiskey bottle, and even a moving van.

Beer is served on the grounds, but you may want to refrain from smoking around the balloons. Also don't grab lines, or you may find yourself part of lift-off. Bring your camera, and wear comfortable shoes. A pilot may ask you to help the crew. Chairs can be rented. And if you decide to drive rather than take the Metro shuttle, plan to arrive early to avoid the crowds.

## Armand Bayou Nature Center

8500 Bay Area Blvd. (located a short distance from Johnson Space Center) • P.O. Box 58828 • Houston, TX 77258 • 281/474-2551
Wed.–Sat. 9 a.m.–5 p.m. • Sat. 12 p.m.–dusk • Closed Mon., Tues.
Adults, $2.50, seniors (62 and older) $1, children (5-17) $1, children (4 and under) and members free. • Group rates available

Considered a Houston area natural treasure, Armand Bayou Nature Center, a living museum on the western shore of Galveston Bay, is a 2,500-acre tract of wilderness that traces Armand Bayou, a natural estuary, and a fin and shellfish nursery for shrimp, crabs, flounder, menhaden, mullet, and other sea life. Alligators linger here and listen as coyotes bay at the moon and swamp rabbits, unaware they are being watched, munch on wild grasses. Naturalists here go to great lengths to protect nature from the ravishes of man and machine. However, more than 70,000 visitors walk here annually along a 500-foot teaching boardwalk where numerous displays and demonstrations bring humans close to fragile ecosystems with elusive wildlife. As visitors stroll, songbirds, such as warblers, flycatchers, orioles and painted buntings, compete with the cries of osprey, owls, kites, and birds-of prey, for audience attention. The walkway ends at the interpretive building where you can get literature about self-guided hikes, canoeing programs, marine biology, ecology, birding, natural history, and special events that often occur at the center. Over 220 species of birds rely on the Nature Center Preserve, a very productive and diverse habitat, as a resting place on their long migratory journeys.

The center has three original major ecosystems: the hardwood bottom land forest, the tall coastal grass prairie, and the estuarine bayou. Considered one of the last undisturbed Texas bayous, hundreds of wildlife species, including those rarely seen such as the bobcat and the owl, thrive in the narrow wooded streams and scattered lakes, ponds, and marshes. Originally known as "Middle Bayou," it was officially renamed in 1970 in memory of Armand Yramategul, a Texas Gulf Coast conservationist and visionary who inspired the drive to preserve this special place. Today, although subsidence is under control, the bayou has lost almost 90 percent of its marshes. Last count revealed 370 species of birds, mammals, reptiles, and amphibians as well as the white-tailed deer, armadillo, poisonous and non-poisonous snakes, turtles, and frogs. The Armand Bayou Nature Center has been designated as one of the only four Texas State Coastal Preserves.

There are strict rules here, however. No pets, picnicking, jogging, running, biking, or radios. Children under 12 must be accompanied by an adult. Don't swat the insects that are part of nature's great scheme, but be sure to wear mosquito repellent.

Special programs include Spring and Fall Migratory Bird Weekends, an annual Earth Day Celebration, Creepy Crawlers Halloween Event, Children's EcoCamps, Farm Day Weekends, monthly Wildlife Focus Special Events, and much, much more. Guided tours are also available throughout the year, as well as Dawn/Dusk/Night Wildlife Observation Walks. Call for schedules.

In December, the center hosts an annual Yuletide Gathering at the Armand Bayou Nature Center's Martyn Farm and an Old-Fashioned Christmas Market, with gifts inspired by nature. The Gathering features a hay wagon ride bedecked with sleigh bells and a campfire singalong of Christmas carols. Adding to the holiday spirit are performances by the Bay Area Symphonic Society and the Clear Lake Metropolitan Ballet.

## Clear Lake Park

3105 NASA Rd. 1 • Seabrook, TX 77586 • 281/333-3334 or 281/488-7676

If you're looking for a serene public park to have a picnic lunch after spending time at NASA, head for Clear Lake Park, a beautiful old shady grove overlooking the lake. After a sandwich, the kids can expend energies on the playground equipment while you feed crumbs to the hungry ducks and geese that show no fear of man or beast.

Once the stomping grounds for the seven-and eight-foot-tall Karankawa Indians, Clear Lake is a favorite of sailors and jet ski enthusiasts as well as those who enjoy relaxing near the water's edge.

## Texas Ice Stadium

**18150 Gulf Fwy. • Houston, TX 77546 • 281/486-7979**
**Admission fee: $5.50 plus $2 for skate rental**

The Texas Ice Stadium is a new 50,000-sq.-ft. public ice skating rink with locker rooms, party/event rooms, pro shop, child care area, restaurant, sports bar, video arcade. Hockey and figure skating events, as well as skating classes, also occur at this facility, which is located north of Baybrook Mall, off I-45 at the Friendswood exit.

## Stardust Trail Rides

**3001 Calder Dr. • League City, TX 77573 • 281/332-9370**
**$20 per hour**

The largest equestrian center in the Gulf Coast area offers a range of trail rides on a 1,000-acre working cattle ranch. A special evening called "Taste of Texas" includes an old-fashioned barbecue, accompanied by a cowboy serenade. Texan Robert Abel, who owns the spread says that since 1991 he has played cowboy host to 90,000 riders.

Group packages include barbecue meals, a petting zoo, sports fields, and hay rides. The "Romantic Adventure" is a ten hour evening in Hideaway Park complete with a bottle of wine, a platter of cheese, a campfire, tent, two horses, and even a personalized copy of Elizabeth Barret Browning's *Sonnet 33*, "How Do I Love Thee." The cost is around $100. To get there, travel south toward Galveston on I-45. Take Exit 22 at League City. Turn right on Calder. The ranch is one mile from freeway.

## Bayou Wildlife Park

**5050 FM 517 • Alvin, TX 77511 • 281/337-6376**

The Bayou Wildlife Ranch ranks among the best wildlife preserves in its class. This 85-acre natural habitat, owned by Clint and Barbara Wolston who are dedicated to preserving endangered species, is the home of over 400 exotic animals, with 35 species represented. From the open-air tram, with running commentary by Clint, you'll see rhinos, Bactrian camels, giraffes, zebras, a Watusi bull, flocks of ostriches, a ring-tail Lemur, a Scimitar Horned Oryx, black swans, a couple of Thanksgiving-size turkeys, and the rare white rhino. Recently, the Wolstons have added an alligator farm and monkey island to their menagerie.

You'll learn facts such as one ostrich egg will fill four cups and camels store water, not in their humps or stomachs, but in the tissues of their bodies. Just south of Clear Lake, 10 miles from NASA. Exit FM 517 off I-45 south, go west 6 miles.

# Houston Raceway Park

281/383-2666 • 2525 FM 565 South • Baytown, TX 77520
$7–$53, depending upon event

The Houston Raceway Park is a national event tract hosting two (NHRA-National Hotrod Association) events each year in March and October, typically the last weekend of each month. One of the country's quickest and fastest ¼-mile drag strips, it seats approximately 30,000. A half million spectators attend park races annually.

Weekly evening races occur on Wednesday, Friday, and Saturday. Feature events occur monthly. Big names, including Eddie Hill, Kenny Bernstein, Joe Amato, and Warren Johnson have raced here. To get to the track from Galveston, travel north on Hwy. 146 and over the Fred Hartman Bridge to FM 565, which is the third light. Make a right going east. The track is 2½ miles down.

# Gulf Greyhound Park

1000 FM 2004 • P.O. Box 488 • LaMarque, TX 77568 • 800/275-2946, 409/986-9500 • Matinee races: Fri.–Sun. with post time at 1:30 p.m. • Evening races: Tues., Thurs.–Sun. with post time at 7:30 p.m. Winning Wednesday: post times 4 p.m. & 7:20 p.m. with 19 races back-to-back • How to get there: Take I-45 south from Houston. Take Exit 15. The track is 30 miles south of Houston and 15 miles north of Galveston

The world's largest greyhound race track, Gulf Greyhound Park is lauded as "the world's biggest dog house." This air-conditioned four-level complex, including Texas' largest full-service restaurant, features pari-mutuel wagering featured year-round, rain or shine, Tues. through Sun. This facility that welcomes families, the park sponsors events every month with many, for example, the Wiener Dog races, that appeal to the younger set. As for greyhound enthusiasts, there's a race every 15 minutes.

If you want to save your money for betting, you can pay only $1 admission to the Plaza and Terrace (Levels 1 & 2), which are air-conditioned and casual. The Players Lounge & Clubhouse (Levels 3 & 4), where admission is only $4, provide a more attractive setting away from the family atmosphere but is still comfortable and casual. The Players Lounge (level 3) offers a "sports bar" atmosphere with first-come, first-serve tables for 500. TV monitors give players close views while teller windows are only a few steps away. On Level 4, the Horizon Clubhouse, players have a great view of the track, and there are TV monitors at each table. The restaurant seats over 1,900 people. Food varies from hamburgers to Mexican food to ice cream.

These sleek greyhounds, who can see up to one-half mile away, spend 75 percent of the race in the air and travel at speeds up to 45 miles per hour. If you want to adopt a retiring greyhound, call the Adoption Program at the Gulf Greyhound Park at 409/986-9500.

# SHOPPING

### Historic League City

East Main St. • League City, TX 77573 • 281/332-1517

First settled in 1855, League City was originally known as Clear Creek. In those days, the only inhabitants were Tejas Indians who had many small villages along the area creeks and waterways. The Karankawas also lived near here and were thought to be cannibalistic although recent research indicates this may not be true. Later during Texas' fight for independence, Santa Anna and his men, in pursuit of Sam Houston, crossed Clear Creek several times. Historians say there are still visible signs on the banks which tell of their crossings. It is also a popular belief that the Mexicans buried treasures and equipment somewhere along the creek. Jean Lafitte also made excursions up the waterways from Galveston, and some believe he, too, buried treasure in the area.

Today, this little community, lined with historic live oaks, has a cluster of antique shops, tea rooms, resale stores, arts and crafts shops, and a bookstore, as well as the West Bay Common School Children's Museum (open by appointment)—all of which are located in historical buildings.

### Factory Stores of America

Exit 13 off I-45 South • La Marque, TX 77568 • 409/938-3333

### Baybrook Mall

500 Baybrook Mall (Bay Area Blvd. and I-45 South) • Friendswood, 77546 • 281/488-4620

# ACCOMMODATIONS

Many of the area hotels and motels offer a special "Bed, Breakfast, Balloons" package, which includes a continental breakfast plus free entrance to the festival.

$ (under $55)

$$ ($55–$75)

$$$ ($75–$125)

$$$$ ($125 and up)

## Nassau Bay Hilton and Marina

3000 NASA Rd. 1 • Houston, TX 77058 • 800/634-4320,
281/333-9300

Scenic high-rise hotel with marina overlooking Clear Lake. Two ballrooms, plus Marina Bar and Grill.

## South Shore Harbour Resort and Conference Center

2500 South Shore Blvd. • League City, TX 77573 • 281/334-1000,
800/442-5005 • $135–$195 (honeymoon suite)

Luxury hotel on Clear Lake, minutes from Space Center Houston, offers 27-hole championship golf course, amphitheater, marina, three restaurants, tropical pool and swim-up bar. 250 rooms. Contract with Clear Lake Charters, including dinner cruises, stargazer evenings, party boats. Water sports available.

## Best Western NASA—Space Center

889 W. Bay Area Blvd. • Webster, TX 77598 • 281/338-6000,
800/528-1234 • $$

## Comfort Inn—Space Center/Houston

750 W. NASA Rd. 1 • Webster, TX 77598 • 281/332-1001,
800/228-5150 • $–$$

## Days Inn—NASA

2020 NASA Rd. 1 • Nassau Bay, TX 77058 • 800-DAYS INN
(329-7466), 281/333-0308 • $

## Holiday Inn Express Hotel and Suites

2720 NASA Rd. 1 • Seabrook, TX 77586 • 281/326-7200,
800/HOLIDAY • $$$

## Holiday Inn NASA

1300 NASA Rd. 1 • Nassue Bay, TX 77058 • 281/333-2500,
800/682-3193 • $$

## Homewood Suites Hotel

4011 Bay Area Blvd. • Houston, TX 77058 • 281/486-7677,
800/CALL HOME • $$$–$$$$

## Marina Park Inn

601 Texas Ave. • Kemah, TX 77565 • 281/334-4855 or
800/437-PARK • $$–$$$$

## Motel 6

11001 W. NASA Rd. 1 • Webster, TX 77598 • 281/332-4581,
800/4MOTEL6 • $, children under 17 free with parents

## Quality INN—NASA

904 E. NASA Rd. 1 • Houston, TX 77058 • 800/228-5151,
281-333-3737 • $

## Ramada Inn/NASA

1301 NASA Rd. 1 • Houston, TX 77058 • 281/488-0220,
800/2RAMADA • $$

## Residence Inn by Marriott

525 Bay Area Blvd. • Houston, TX 77058 • 281/486-2424,
800/331-3131 • $$$$

## Super 8 Motel—NASA

18103 Kings Row • Houston, TX 77058 • 281/333-5385,
800/800-8000 • $

## Super 8 Motel—League City

102 Hobbs Rd. • League City, TX 77573 • 281/338-0800,
800/800-8000 • $

# RESTAURANTS

## Cavanagh's

803 E. NASA Rd. 1 • Webster, TX 77598 • 281/488-6300

## Cross-Eyed Seagull

1010 E. NASA RD. 1 • Webster, TX 77598 • 281/333-3488

## Jalapeño Tree

316 W. NASA Rd. 1 • Webster, TX 77598 • 281/332-5502

## Perry's Grille

487 Bay Area Blvd. • Houston, TX 77058 • 281/286-8800

## Tommy's Patio Cafe
2555 Bay Area Blvd. • Houston, TX 77058 • 281/474-3444

## China Square
1111 E. NASA Rd. 1 • Webster, TX 77598 • 281/486-7722

## Szechuan Garden
707 W. Main • League City, TX 77573 • 281/332-1618

## Enzo's
720 W. NASA Rd. 1 • Webster, TX 77598 • 281/332-6955

## Laura's Tea Room
2339 Bay Area Blvd. • Houston, TX 77058 • 281/480-1600

## Frenchie's
1041 E. NASA Rd. 1 • Webster, TX 77598 • 281/486-7144

## Mamacita's
515 E. NASA Rd. 1 • Webster, TX 77598 • 281/332-5362

## Pappasito's
20099 I-45 South • Webster, TX 77598 • 281/338-2885

# AREA LIBRARIES

## Mares Memorial Library
## Galveston County Library System
4324 Hwy. 3 • Dickinson, TX 77539 • 713/534-3812 • Closed
Sunday

## Friendswood Public Library
416 S. Friendswood Dr. • Friendswood, TX 77546 • 713/482-7135
Closed Sunday

## Hitchcock Public Library
Genevieve Miller Library • 8005 Barry St. • Hitchcock, TX 77563
409/986-7814 • Closed Sunday

## La Marque Public Library

1011 Bayou Rd. • La Marque, TX 77568 • 409/938-9270
Closed Sunday

## League City Public Library
## Helen Hall Library

100 West Walker • League City, TX 77573 • 713/338-4860

## Moore Memorial Library

1701 9th Ave. N • Texas City, TX 77590 • 409/643-5979

## Santa Fe Public Library

Mae S. Bruce Library • P.O. Box 950 • 13302 6th St.
Santa Fe, TX 77510 • 409/925-5540

# SEABROOK AND KEMAH

## Seabrook Chamber of Commerce

### 1201 East NASA Rd. 1 • Seabrook, TX • 281/488-7676

Kemah, "the gateway to the bay," nestled in a half-moon pocket on Galveston Bay, is experiencing a major facelift, thanks to Landry's Seafood Restaurants, Inc. The picturesque Kemah Waterfront is destined to become a 14-acre entertainment complex and boardwalk that will include theme restaurants, shops, a first-class hotel, a specialty aquarium restaurant, a water garden, and family amusements. A boardwalk and a major pedestrian corridor will link all together. Founded in 1898 by John Henry Kipp, veteran of the Magnolia Rangers, Kemah offers a premiere marina, day-sail and fishing expeditions, quality seafood restaurants, quaint retail shops, galleries, and antique shops.

Old Seabrook became a townsite in 1895. In 1930, the highway bridge was built to take the place of a hand-cranked ferry boat that sailed between Seabrook and Kemah. In 1961, the year Hurricane Carla hit and almost wiped out the city, NASA announced its location 3 miles from Seabrook. Today, it is a quaint little community destined for recognition.

Seabrook, an art and antique seaside colony that neighbors Kemah, is flanked by both Galveston Bay and Clear Lake. Both seaside retreats are a sailor's paradise with three major marinas and the Lakewood Yacht Club— one of the top ten yacht clubs in America. Land lovers, though, also love the area, not only for the constant parade of vessels that travel the channel that undercuts the Kemah/Seabrook Bridge, but also for the colorful enclave of restaurants, shops, and seafood markets that make these coastal towns so picturesque. Visit here, and you're 20 miles from the Gulf Greyhound Racing Park and the Lone Star Outlet Mall.

Here in Kemah and Seabrook you'll find the best seafood dining around. To get there, go south on I-45 to the FM 518 exit. Go east (left) on FM 518 to FM 2094. Continue east on FM 2094 to Hwy. 146. On the right of the Kemah/Seabrook Bridge is Kemah. On the left is Seabrook.

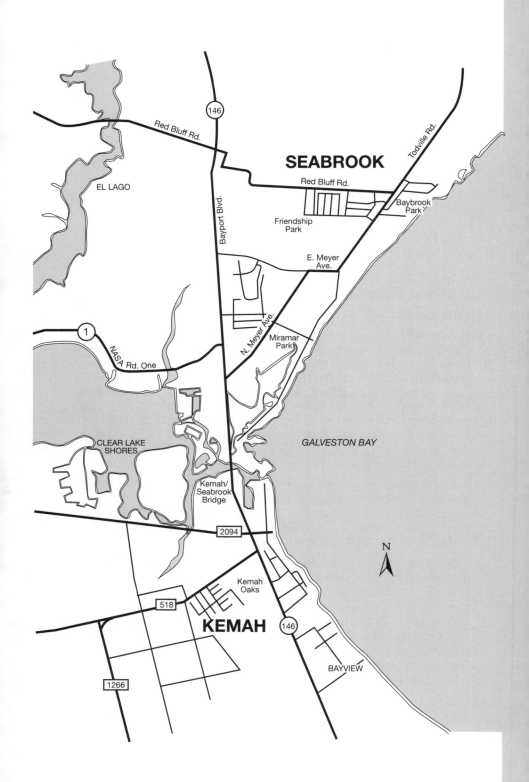

# RESTAURANTS

Many of the restaurants listed here are along the Kemah-Seabrook channel that lines the waterfront district, where you can watch the parade of sailboats and yachts going to and from Clear Lake and Galveston Bay while you dine. There is also a boat basin here as well as places where you can buy fresh seafood.

### Key to Symbols

$          Inexpensive/under $7
$$         Moderate/$7–$15
$$$        Expensive/$16–$29
$$$$       Very Expensive/$30 and up

*All prices are subject to change. They reflect dinner for one, exclusive of liquor, tax, and tip.*

## Landry's Seafood Restaurant

**201 Kipp • 281/334-2513 • Kemah, TX 77565 • $$–$$$**

Formerly Jimmie Walker's, Landry's is located directly on the water as the cut opens to the bay. On pleasant days, there is a constant parade of private vessels that make their way into open water. Ask for a table by a window so you'll have a good view. The seafood is excellent.

## Pappadeaux's Seafood Kitchen

**309 Waterfront Dr. • Seabrook, TX 77586 • 281/291-9932 $$–$$$$**

A bay-side restaurant owned by the Pappas family, Houston's popular restaurant family, Pappadeaux's features seafood cooked Cajun style. You can't get any better than the fresh fish, shrimp, and crabs prepared here.

## The Crab House

**Waterfront Dr. and Todville Rd. • Kemah, TX 77565 281/474-5836 • $$**

A great experience for sea lovers. Dine on steamed crabs and shrimp served on newspaper as you watch the parade of sailboats.

## S. W. Tookie's

**1202 Route 146 (Bayport Blvd.) • Seabrook, TX 77586 281/474-3444 • $**

## Villa Capri
37134 NASA Rd. 1 • Seabrook, TX • 281/326-2373

## Seabrook Classic Cafe
2511 NASA Rd. 1 • Seabrook, TX • 281/326-1512

## Crazy Cajun
2825 NASA Rd. 1 • Seabrook, TX • 281/326-6055

Here you'll get the best hamburgers you have ever eaten. They're marinated in wine, and Tookie's even grinds its own meat. This restaurant has been in business for years and is a favorite among locals who strongly recommend #99, a ground round hamburger marinated in port.

# ACCOMMODATIONS

## Captain's Quarters
701 Bay Ave. • Kemah, TX 77565 • 281/334-414121

This five-star elegant waterside bed and breakfast, has made the pages of *Southern Living* and *Texas Highways*. A New England-styled sea captain's home with a view of Galveston Bay, this five-level 19th century structure is a spacious 8,500 square feet. The grand stairway leads to upper levels, the top one a widow's walk. A private pier lends well to an afternoon drink as the sun sets over the water. Guests may use the nearby yacht club pool and tennis courts and moor their vessels at the marina. A full gourmet breakfast is served.

## Crew's Quarters
114 Waterfront Dr. • Seabrook, TX • 281/334-4141

The Crew's Quarters, a quaint historic seaside retreat on Galveston Bay, is in Kemah across from Captain's Quarters. Located where the channel and the bay join and perched on pilings, this summer place has been in the owner's family for 50 years.

Each room is nautical and painted in seaside colors. Breakfast specialties include Scotch eggs, fried shredded wheat, and special cinnamon coffee. Guests may use the nearby yacht club pool and tennis courts and moor their vessels at the marina.

Stay here and you'll be in shouting distance to passing sailboats that make their way into the bay.

# 1874 Kipp House

P.O. Box 975 • Kemah, TX 77565 • 281/334-3474 • $$$$
Two suites, gourmet breakfast, no children, no pets, smoking in
designated areas

Built by a sea captain and the founder of Kemah, John Kipp, this excep-
tionally kept bay home whispers of affluence, seafaring strength, and good
taste. Now owned by businessman Matt Wiggins, also grandson to
Kemah's restaurateur Jimmy Walker, this bed and breakfast, with richly
varnished walls, oriental carpeted floors, and comfortable, yet elegant, furnishings, provides a panoramic view of Galveston Bay.

Matt has added personal touches, however, that reveal his wide range of
interests. Visitors here can't decide what to admire first—his original
Audubon prints, his nautical memorabilia or his collection of gaming
tables and other items taken from Galveston and Kemah gambling houses
once alive but illegal during a time long gone. Be sure to note the European roulette wheel with the absent "double O," so indicative of the American ones. Also inspect the original "floating" Galveston County crap table,
designed to make quick getaways from gun-toting Texas Rangers.

This unhosted B&B doesn't lack for a gourmet breakfast either. Guests
walk just across the street to Mary Patterson's Captain's Quarters, where
everyone sits at a crystal- and china-laden dining table for fruit, scrambled
eggs, and sausage-filled rolls.

# The Pelican House Bed and Breakfast

1302 First St. • Seabrook, TX 77586 • 281/474-5295
FAX 281/474-7840 • $$–$$$$ (depending on number of rooms or
whole house rental) • Full breakfast, children over 10 only, no pets,
smoking in designated areas

Just footsteps away from Seabrook's Back Bay Lagoon, a charming little
yellow house has made a local name for itself as one of the most endearing
spots in town. The Pelican House, a 90-year-old one-story home owned
by the first area school teacher, sits on over an acre shaded with pecan and
live oak trees. There's nothing fancy here but porch rockers and a tree
swing for two to lull away city pressures. In view is the lazy bay, home of
herons, pelicans, and the hawk-like osprey. Hours seem like minutes as
one watches the waterbirds dive for their breakfast. In the distance, a
rooster crows "Good morning!" and Schooner, a neighbor's parrot, giggles,
"Help me!"

The decor is arty, with sea murals painted by local artists and clay
pieces, created by the potter who lives in the garage apartment out back.
The main motif is the gangly old pelican. Suzanne Silver, a hostess with
personality-plus, comes in for breakfast and prepares such specialties as a
Sunday Stuffed French toast with pepper bacon and apricot glaze or morn-
ing crepes. Wine, ice tea, or champagne welcomes guests. Fishing and
crabbing is in walking distance. Bring your gear.

## The Ark

705 6th St. • Kemah, TX 77565 • 281/474-5295
FAX 281/474-7840 • $$$–$$$$ (depending on number of rooms
or whole house rental), children over 10 only, no pets, smoking in
designated areas

The Ark is a three-bedroom, two-bath bay house that overlooks Galveston Bay. Decorated with a nautical theme in foam greens, pale tans, sea blues, and warm reds, the furnishings definitely have a decorator's touch. But the most impressive feature is its deck that reaches toward the beautiful Galveston Bay. In fact, from the side windows, one can see the distant sailboats as they make their way into the channel that leads to the Kemah/Seabrook Bridge.

Under the house is a ten-person hot tub, stereo speakers, a patio area, and access to the water via a small pier where crabs and speckled trout await your bait. With no host present, the gourmet continental breakfast is self-serve. The table sits twelve.

# SHOPPING

Every second Saturday and Sunday of the month, Old Seabrook (NASA Rd. 1 and Hwy. 146, 281/474-3869) hosts their "Back Bay Market," a walkabout that takes visitors to almost 30 shops, including such antique shops as **Another Era** (909 Hardesty, 281/474-7208) and **The Victorian Rose** (909 Hall, 281/474-1214). If you're in the market for natural foods, try the **Old Seabrook Spice Company** (Hwy. 146 and Hardesty St., 281/474-2417), a combination store and restaurant that is sure to keep you healthy. For handmade items, try the **Homespun Arts and Crafts Mall** (2200 Bayport, 281/474-3303) or the **Texas General Store** (2200A Bayport, 281/474-2882). If you're in the market for a flag or kite, drop by the **Money Makers** (1425 Hwy. 146, 281/474-1200), for flags, banners, windsox, kites, flag poles, custom flags, and screen printing.

On the Kemah side, you can find seashells at such places as **The Shell Boutique** (505 Bradford, 281/538-4457) where you can also shop for Texas Gourmet foods and coffees. Find organic cotton clothing at **Natural Things** (505 Bradford/upstairs, 281/334-4802). If you like gifts and prints with the nautical flair, walk over to **Kemah Ketch,** 509 Bradford, 281/334-5611. Are you a cigar smoker? Plan to spend some time at **Churchill's at Downing Street,** 709 Bradford, 281/334-6325, where owners say, "It's better to light a cigar than curse the darkness!" For an unusual shopping experience, try **Eg-quisit Egg Shells** (605 6th St., 281/538-4165) where you can purchase decorated eggshells, musical and mechanical eggs, stained glass, pottery, jewelry by local artists and Boardwalk fudge. For a beer, try **Captain George's Coffee Shop** and **Longboat Pub** (606 6th "A" St., 281/334-7803). In all, Kemah boasts almost 100 businesses.

# BRAZOSPORT

## Brazosport Area Chamber of Commerce

420 Hwy. 332 W • Brazosport, TX 77531 • 409/265-2505
Fax: 409/265-4246

On Galveston's southwest across San Luis Pass, the Brazosport area is comprised of nine small cities including Freeport, Surfside Beach, Clute, Jones Creek, Lake Jackson, Richwood, Quintana, and Oyster Creek. A land rich with natural resources, this coastal region offers miles of free sandy beaches, jetty fishing, and campgrounds. Surfside Beach is a 21-mile stretch of unspoiled coastline that is a favorite of sun worshipers who prefer a more private commune with nature. As for West Bay, it's a fisherman's paradise that is also a find for birdwatchers—in fact, southern Brazoria County has been ranked No. 1 in the annual Christmas Bird Count more than 14 times in the past two decades. That's because the Brazoria, San Bernard, and Big Boggy national wildlife refuges are all located in this coastal area.

Located in southern Brazoria County 50 miles southwest of Houston, Freeport is the place to go if you love to fish, crab, bird watch, beachcomb, deep-sea fish, or scuba dive. A haven for red fish, flounder, and speckled trout, fishermen marvel as brown pelicans crisscross each other as they dive-bomb mullet that innocently meander just under the surface.

## Birds of Brazosport

In 1993, the Texas Department of Transportation received federal funding to pay for the development of The Great Texas Coastal Birding Trail. There are 96 sites that make up the trails' central section, which extends more than 200 miles, from Sargent Beach near Freeport southward to the Louise Trant Bird Sanctuary near Riviera. The Brazoria Refuge Complex was recently designated as an internationally significant shorebird site by the Western Hemisphere Shorebird Reserve Network. The Brazoria, San Bernard, and Big Boggy complexes provide sanctuary for more than 300 species of birds during the winter months. Large concentrations of up to

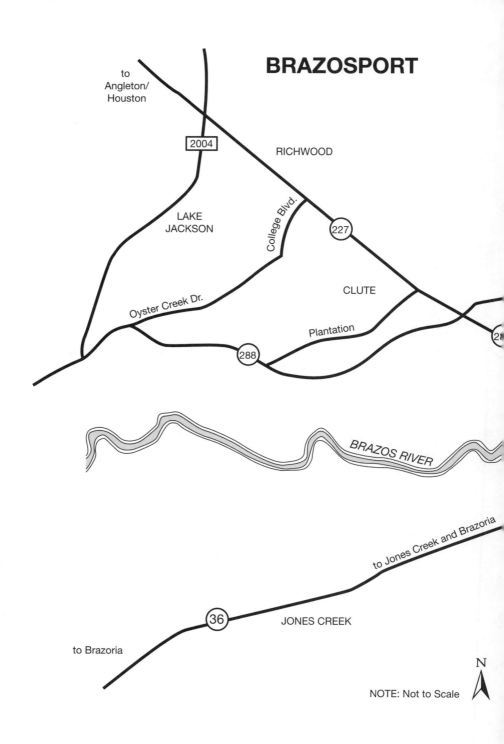

# BRAZOSPORT

to
Angleton/
Houston

2004

RICHWOOD

LAKE
JACKSON

College Blvd.

227

CLUTE

Oyster Creek Dr.

Plantation

28

288

BRAZOS RIVER

to Jones Creek and Brazoria

36   JONES CREEK

to Brazoria

N

NOTE: Not to Scale

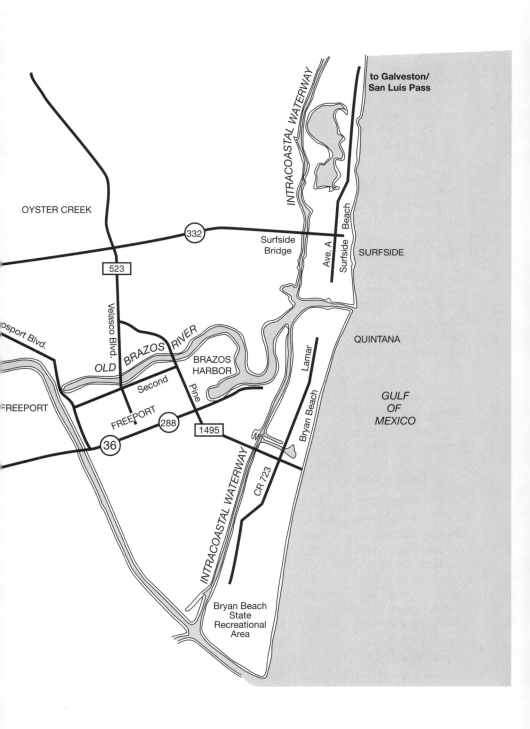

OYSTER CREEK

to Galveston/
San Luis Pass

INTRACOASTAL WATERWAY

332

Surfside
Bridge

523

Ave. A

Surfside Beach

SURFSIDE

Velasco Blvd.

OLD BRAZOS RIVER

osport Blvd.

QUINTANA

BRAZOS
HARBOR

Second

Pine

Lamar

GULF
OF
MEXICO

FREEPORT

FREEPORT

288

1495

Bryan Beach

36

INTRACOASTAL WATERWAY

CR 723

Bryan Beach
State
Recreational
Area

100,000 geese and 80,000 ducks make their home here. Birdwatchers also see an additional 50 migrant bird varieties beginning in March and ending in mid-May. Among the many feathered friends to come here are the songbirds, wading birds, warblers, scissor-tailed flycatchers, eastern wood-pewees and kingbirds, and Louisiana waterthrushes.

A few other well-known birding areas in Brazoria county include the bird sanctuary on Quintana Beach, Wilderness Park in Lake Jackson, Brazos Bend State Park, Hanson Riverside County Park in West Columbia, Freeport Municipal Park, and Peach Point Wildlife Management Area in Jones Creek.

The annual Migration Celebration, which occurs the last week of April and first week of May, includes speakers, tours, and field trips. For more on this and birding sites, contact the Brazosport Chamber of Commerce or 800/938-4853. For tours, call Texas Nature Adventures, 800/268-7289.

## Sea Center Texas

Lake Jackson • Hwy. 332 • 300 Medical Dr. • Lake Jackson, TX 77566 409/292-0100 • Free • Tues.–Fri., 9 a.m.–4 p.m., Sat., 10 a.m.–5 p.m., Sun., 1 p.m.–4 p.m. • Closed Mon.

Recently opened, Sea Center Texas is a combination marine aquarium, fish hatchery, and Visitors Center. The $12-million facility, created in partnership with Dow Chemical, the Gulf Coast Conservation Association, and the Texas Parks and Wildlife Department, features interpretive displays, two "touch tanks," two 2,500-gallon aquariums, two 5,000-gallon aquariums, and one 52,000-gallon aquarium, where a 300-pound grouper and a school of sharks watch as visitors come to call.

Tours of the hatchery are indeed an education, but be sure to make reservations first.

## The Brazosport Center for Arts and Sciences

400 College Dr. • Lake Jackson, TX 77566 • 409/265-7661

The center promotes the appreciation of art, natural science, theater, nature, and music. Live theater productions occur here on the Brazosport Center Stages, which has the oldest theater group on the Texas Coast. Also featured are workshops, symphony performances, art classes, a museum, a planetarium, art gallery, and the largest seashell collection in the south, displayed in the Hall of Malacology. The Nature Center and Planetarium provides educational programs throughout the year, and visitors can take a self-guided tour along the banks of Oyster Creek on the nature trail.

## Gulf Water Diving

Some diving enthusiasts say that offshore from these coastal cities are some of the best underwater attractions anywhere. The Stetson Bank and Flower Garden Bank are the top two attractions off the Texas coast at 70 miles and 100 miles, respectively. The naturally formed coral wreaths and clear water attract many varieties of sea creatures. Schools of manta rays and hammerhead sharks like to accompany divers as they examine the wondrous colors found in underwater formations. On occasion, the rate whale shark, ranging from 12 to 35 ft. long, appears to startle visitors. At the Stetson garden, you'll see the same fish you would encounter in the Atlantic and the Caribbean.

Dive boats carry up to 34 passengers on three- and four-day trips. Bed linens and meals are included on the boats. According to locals, the best time to plan a diving trip is between July and September. Call the Brazosport Chamber of Commerce for details.

# ACCOMMODATIONS

## BED AND BREAKFASTS

### Anchor Bed and Breakfast

342 Anchor Dr. (Treasure Island) • Freeport, TX 77541
409/239-3543

### Bankers Inn Bed and Breakfast

224 W. Park Ave. • Freeport, TX 77541 • 409/233-4932

### Roses and the River

7074 CR 506• Brazosport, TX 77422 • 800/610-1070 or
409/798-1070

## HOTELS/MOTELS

### Anchor Motel

1302 Blue Water Hwy. • Surfside Beach, TX 77541 • 409/239-3543

### Best Western Lake Jackson Inn

915 Hwy. 332 • Lake Jackson, TX 77566 • 409/297-3031

### Cedar Sands Motel

343 N. Beachfront • Surfside Beach • P.O. Box 942 • Freeport, TX
77542 • 409/233-1942

## Country Hearth Inn
1015 W. Second St. • Freeport, TX 77541 • 409/239-1602

## Days Inn
805 W. Hwy. 332 • P.O. Box 66 • Clute, TX 77531 • 409/265-3301

## Holiday Inn Express
809 W. Hwy. 332 • Clute, TX 77531 • 409/265-5252

## La Quinta Motor Inn
1126 Hwy. 332 • Clute, TX 77531 • 409/265-7461

## Ramada Inn, Lake Jackson
925 Hwy. 332 • Lake Jackson, TX 77566 • 409/297-1161

## Surfside Motel
330 Coral Ct. • Surfside Beach, TX 77541 • 409/233-4585

# RESTAURANTS

## Dolce Vita
145 Oyster Creek Dr. • Lake Jackson, TX 77566 • 409/299-0008

## Cafe Loredo
403 This Way • Hwy. 332 • Lake Jackson, TX 77566 • 409/297-0696

## Cactus Grill
107 West Way, Suite 7 • Lake Jackson, TX 77566 • 409/285-9300

## Garfield's Restaurant and Pub
100 W. Hwy. 332 #1362 • Lake Jackson, TX 77566 • 409/297-3993

## Kettle Country Cafe
917 Hwy. 332 W. • Lake Jackson, TX 77566 • 409/297-9354

## On the River Restaurant
919 W. 2nd. St. • Freeport, TX 77541 • 409/233-0503

## Potatoe Patch Restaurant

919 W. Hwy. 332 • Clute, TX 77531 • 409/265-4285

## Red Snapper Inn

402 Bluewater Hwy. • Surfside Beach, TX 77541 • 409/239-3226

## Smithhart's Downtown Grill

104 That Way • Lake Jackson, TX 77566 • 409/297-0082

## Windswept Seafood Restaurant

105 Burch Circle, Oyster Creek • Freeport, TX 77542
409/233-1951

# INDEX